Confronting Crisis:

Teachers in America

"If teaching and learning have a practical goal . . . , it is this: to keep the men who run our national plant from being run by it— that is, to keep them men, or better, to keep them artists."

Jacques Barzun

Confronting Crisis:

Edited and with
an introduction by

Illustrations by

Teachers in America

Ernestine P. Sewell
& Billi M. Rogers

Harry Hanks

The University of Texas
at Arlington Press 1979

Acknowledgments

Acknowledgment is made to the following for permissions to print:

The College English Association, Inc., for "Working Words" by Richard B. Sewall, copyright 1977. Reprinted from *The CEA Critic*, 1977; abridgment of "Forty Years of *Understanding Poetry*," by Cleanth Brooks, copyright 1979. Permissions of Richard B. Sewall and Cleanth Brooks.

The Texas College English Association for abridgment of "Can These Bones Live—and Should They?" by James Sledd, 1978. Permission of James Sledd.

Hazard Adams for quotation in "Forty Years of *Understanding Poetry*" by Cleanth Brooks. Reprinted from *The Interests of Criticism.*

Jacques Barzun for quotation from *Teacher in America,* copyright 1954 by Jacques Barzun. Reprinted from *Teacher in America*, Doubleday 1954.

Dwight L. Bolinger for revision of "Let's Change Our Base of Operations," copyright 1969 by Dwight L. Bolinger. Permission of *Modern Language Journal.*

Haldref Publications for revision of "The Lights Men Live By" by Maxwell H. Goldberg, copyright 1977. Reprinted from *Improving College and University Teaching*. Permission of Maxwell H. Goldberg.

Nova, The University of Texas at El Paso, for revision of "The Folklore of Academe," by C. Leland Sonnichsen, June 1973. Permission of C. Leland Sonnichsen.

Jesse Stuart for abridgment of "To Teach, To Love," copyright 1972 by Jesse Stuart. Reprinted from *To Teach, To Love*, Bantam 1972.

Contents

Introduction   1

The State of Writing Today   7
    Jacques Barzun

To Make Literature of Our Lives   29
    William A. Owens

Working Words   41
    Richard B. Sewall

The Folklore of Academe   51
    C. L. Sonnichsen

Can These Bones Live—And Should They?   63
    James Sledd

View from a Room in the Ivory Tower   75
    Ruth Z. Temple

Grumble, Grumble, Toil or Tumble   91
    Lewis Leary

No Better Gift of Fortune   101
    Dorothy B. Loomis

The Furnished Mind   113
    Paul W. Barrus

The Lights Men Live By   119
    Maxwell H. Goldberg

A Separate Peace   129
    Waldo F. McNeir

The Politics of Survival   *143*
        William Fulbright

Cats in Air-Pumps   *149*
        Alice R. Bensen

Let's Change Our Base of Operations   *155*
        Dwight L. Bolinger

Forty Years of "Understanding Poetry"   *167*
        Cleanth Brooks

Integrate or Perish   *179*
        Joe D. Thomas

An Abecedarian: from Jocassee to Brooklyn   *187*
        Margaret M. Bryant

Make Haste Slowly   *195*
        C. Richard Sanders

To Teach, To Love   *207*
        Jesse Stuart

The Last Best Hope for Quality
in Higher Education   *223*
        Kenneth H. Ashworth

Introduction

Soon after the publication of *Simple and Direct*, Jacques Barzun, America's eminent cultural historian, accepted an invitation to address teachers, students, and friends at The University of Texas at Arlington. Denouncing the present sad state of education, he exhorted students to accept good writing as the ultimate test of their education, as the evidence of minds disciplined for thinking. Such a standard, Barzun said, could only be met by teachers trained for the specialized job of teaching composition and students who consent to the responsibility for learning to write well.

From the same dais, following Jacques Barzun, William A. Owens, his associate of many years at Columbia University, directed the attention of the audience to the necessity for improved teacher training to break "the chain of errors" perpetrated on education by teachers who themselves are not writers. Rather, he said, they are "jargon makers, self-styled activists, and would-be literary elitists." Drawing on his own experience in writing and teaching writing, Owens urged writers to invoke their experiences as a valid source for "material that can be added to, taken from, distorted to arrive at truth, at universality."

1

The event was unique. The audience responded enthusiastically, as if inspirited by the wisdom and great good humor of the authentic voices that had spoken.

A short time later, it was the good fortune of the editors to hear Richard Sewall raise some difficult questions for the consideration of an audience of college professors, whom he wanted to be "haunted, plagued, and dogged." How much of what is presented in the classroom, he asked, really stays with the students as touchstones for their intellectual, ethical, and emotional needs in the years beyond college?

These three notable addresses, then, seemed to present a charge. Convinced that educators of long experience could address themselves powerfully to the present crisis in our colleges and universities, we determined to collect essays that would record a crucial period in the intellectual life of this country. Thus we extended our invitation to men and women of achievement in the academic world and their responses prove that they are willing and eager to speak boldly about the deterioration of quality in higher education. Their reviews of the past half century are an index of the major issues confronting our colleges and universities: whom shall we teach? what and how shall we teach? how may the university maintain disinterestedness? what are the ethical responsibilities of the teacher? what are the parameters of tenure? how may academic freedom be assured? how shall we prepare teachers to teach?

The consensus of these essayists is that the university must become more self critical, that the ills of the profession must be healed from within, and that the future must be vested in the teacher.

It came as no surprise that disillusion with academia found many voices.

Leland Sonnichsen, editor of the *Arizona Historical Journal*, takes his associates to task in "The Folklore of Academe." Sonnichsen denies that he is "violently anti-professor," claiming "Some of them are my best friends. I don't think . . . that I would want my daughter to marry one, and if I had to be cast ashore on a desert island, and were looking for a suitable person to be cast away with, it would not be a professor." Decrying a new breed of professors who want top money for a minimum teaching load,

2

he nevertheless provides them with a scathing list of commandments for the "business of productive scholarship." Equally outraged, James Sledd scarifies "a profession which has forgot to teach the people knowledge." He excoriates the "comfortable struldbrugs" of the faculty and "the machinery of deans and chairmen and committees and councils and lobbies and newsletters and conventions."

The word *decline* establishes the tone of Ruth Z. Temple's essay, as she speaks from the vantage of more than fifty years in her profession. The declines she views with alarm are in the fortunes of women in the academic world, in the quality of American education, and in standards of taste in the arts. "In the Academy as in the polis, the sleep of reason breedeth monsters," she warns.

Lewis Leary describes himself as "a not completely unscarred veteran of academic warfare" and "unashamedly a grumbler." He calls for housecleaning from within to remove deadwood from tenured positions, to halt the exploitation of teaching assistants, to discriminate between petty and significant publication, to eliminate busyness. "The house of intellect inherited from the past waits to be repaired, new additions added, the roof raised, the cellar deepened, the doorway widened," Leary concludes.

Dorothy Loomis suggests an essential step in repairing Leary's (and Jacques Barzun's) house of intellect: a renewal of the teacher's commitment to both teaching and research. She sees them as handmaidens to serve the prime obligation of furnishing the minds of students. Paul W. Barrus echoes his concern in "The Furnished Mind": "There is no more poignant human tragedy than to approach maturity with an unfurnished mind, a mind that has no resources in itself, a mind that has depended for its sustenance upon passing fads and physical prowess." If his essay sounds the concern of a Jeremiah, his plea for academic commitment to furnishing minds is concluded in tones of sweet calm.

Against the background of holocaust, Maxwell Goldberg has framed the question, what causes one person to crumble and another to strengthen under personal blows? In response to his own query, he derives answers from his own family, his ex-

3

perience, and from literature to discover what lights men live by. Against a disruptive background of another sort Waldo F. McNeir acted out the major drama of his career when he took his stand in favor of Civil Rights. "When I exercised my rights as a citizen and wrote to my state representatives urging them to act like enlightened statesmen, or to assume a virtue if they had it not," McNeir recalls, "my letters were made public, and the hurricane that followed blew away all semblance of reason."

Turning to the how-and-what to teach are essays by William Fulbright, Alice Bensen, Dwight Bolinger, and Cleanth Brooks. Senator Fulbright reiterates his conviction that we can have a better world through education that expands cultural awareness of the peoples of the world. Bensen finds the teacher central to quality education, as she issues a beguiling invitation to enjoy literature: "Fodor and the phrasebook may turn out to be less important preparations for Europe than *Les Miserables* . . . or *War and Peace*." The place of foreign language in the curriculum is the focus of Dwight Bolinger, who proposes some startling innovations in the choice of languages to be taught in the schools. To provide programs for bilingual, bicultural Americans, Bolinger suggests the chosen language be that spoken by a sizable minority in a given community, thus engaging English-speaking students in a foreign-language learning process while lending prestige to the native language of the speakers as they learn English. The name of Cleanth Brooks is almost synonymous with *Understanding Poetry*, so closely intertwined is his career with the "launching and subsequent fortunes of this odd little craft." The book, conceived in response to what Brooks and Robert Penn Warren recognized as needs of their students, has fundamentally changed the teaching of literature, writes Hazard Adams: "It has not and will not return to its former state."

Joe D. Thomas says we must establish a more meaningful continuum from high school to college: "We must integrate our curricula, or we shall perish." Thomas predicts no end to open admissions and inevitable developments to educate an entire populace.

Three outstanding teacher-scholar-writers, Margaret Bryant, Richard Sanders, and Jesse Stuart, have contributed

4

reflections of their careers, in which can be read models for good teaching and a note of hope that education can right itself when, not if, education is vested in faculty. Stuart recreates an image of the one-room school house, to which he would not have us return, but to whose spirit he would have us rally.

Kenneth H. Ashworth, in *American Higher Education in Decline* (1979) has written: "It is ironic that our colleges and universities, the social sciences, behavior, and ways to predict the future, give so little attention to the study of their own past and the social processes at work upon them. . . . The university community probably spends less time studying itself than it does almost any other topic available for scholars to contemplate" (p. 19). In summarizing the concerns of the essayists represented within this book, he concludes that "the faculty is the last best hope for maintaining quality and defining the correct purposes for institutions of higher learning."

We believe this collection of essays confronts the crisis in higher education with such candor as to inspire the American people — students, teachers, and friends of education — to insist upon ameliorative programs that will generate the excellence to which the achievements of these writers attest.

Ernestine P. Sewell and Billi M. Rogers
The University of Texas at Arlington
Arlington, Texas, 1979

Jacques Barzun, born in France, November 30, 1907, was educated in Paris and at Columbia University, New York, where he remained as professor, dean of graduate faculties, and provost until his move to the world of publishers. A Phi Beta Kappan, Barzun is representative of The American Scholar, his writings encompassing art, music, and history from the Classic period through the Romantic to the Modern. His concerns for education are reflected in *Teacher in America, The House of Intellect, The Modern Researcher,* and *Simple and Direct.*

Jacques Barzun

The State
of Writing Today

At almost any other time, the topic assigned to me in this symposium would have been ambiguous. The "State of Writing Today" might have meant the condition of literature — how good are our poets, how numerous and strong our novelists? But these days there is no ambiguity; everybody knows at once that what is meant is the ability of the people at large to express their needs and thoughts on paper — to do so at least well enough to be understood. And the reason we know this to be our topic today is that for two or three years past, the quality of ordinary writing and the teaching of writing in school and college have been discussed and decried.

A well-known television figure has helped give notoriety to the subject in a best-selling book and subsequent lectures. Many horror stories about writing have appeared in the syndicated press. Periodicals ranging from *Harper's, Time* and *Newsweek*, to the educational and other quarterlies have raised their voices in alarm at the trend toward national incoherence. The broadcast hearings about Watergate gave everybody a taste of the ultimate verbal mush and raised widespread doubt as to how government at the very top could be carried on in the darkness of thought disclosed in the memos and reports circulating within the White

7

Confronting Crisis

House. All this concern gave strength to other causes of disquiet about the schools — the repeated drop in S.A.T. scores, the widening gap between mental age and reading ability, the general practice of "social promotion," getting the child out of one grade and into the next regardless of performance.

Suddenly, awareness turned to action and the movement known as Back to Basics was in being from coast to coast. We are here today because of it. Its principle was first enunciated some twenty years ago, when a small independent group of observers formed in Washington the Council for Basic Education and began to deal with the bad teaching of reading. Their efforts turned that tide, so that the look-and-say system, with its use of a limited vocabulary, is being beaten back in favor of the common-sense system of phonics, which opens up to the child an unlimited vocabulary. This change, as I shall hope to show, is all-important to our subject of writing. Reading and writing are bound together like Siamese twins. With counting, they are obviously the basics of the basics.

Their neglect is the reason why the very idea of our school system is in jeopardy and why we have had proposals for de-schooling society. In belated panic, state legislatures have been passing laws demanding that the high school diploma regain some discoverable meaning. For after twelve years of school attendance a pupil may be graduated with a sixth, seventh, or eighth grade level of achievement. Some, indeed, are performing at what can only be called an underground level and add their numbers to the official count of twenty-three million functional illiterates — so called because they cannot function. One of them is at this moment suing his school district in New York State for five million dollars in damages, claiming "educational malpractice."

As for colleges, we all know what a burden of remedial work they have been carrying for years. The system of "open admissions," set up to prove our democratic stand on educational opportunity, has shown that our boasted universal literacy is a fraud: an appalling proportion of those who find themselves in college turn out functional illiterates within that no longer demanding intellectual environment. This is true not only of those handicapped in early years by poverty and feckless

8

schools; it is equally true of those admitted from excellent schools to our leading universities.

Within the last three days the newspapers of Fort Worth and Dallas have carried three news stories on the same point: the first is about the Berkeley-California Writing Project. Instructors at the university there wonder whether "in an age of TV and telephones" it is "still necessary to be able to write an essay." They are determined to find out and are doing so by asking shopkeepers and business executives whether their employees have to write.

The second item is a declaration by a professor at the Southern Methodist University that its graduates know about Plato, but that it is a question whether they can read and write.

And third comes a new notion in college architecture, from the president of Georgetown University in Washington. "The time has come," he says, "to erect a great wall across the middle of the sophomore year, to show that unless you can read and write and do both well, you shall not pass."

Other institutions share the alarm. Harvard has just appropriated over a quarter-million dollars to stop the plague of bad writing, which has apparently broken out of the isolation ward known as remedial courses. Yale professors are clamoring against the bright inarticulate minds they are asked to teach. The faculty of the City University of New York has passed a resolution enabling them to keep out of their classes students who cannot write a simple sentence, in either Spanish or English, and who cannot do simple arithmetic in one of those languages. Cornell University has taken the most desperate step and appointed a Dean of Writing — the first of this kind — given him a million dollars and, I imagine, insured his life for an equal sum.

If I seem to be laughing at these heroic measures, it is only in order not to cry. How far indeed have we come from the faith of our ancestors of a century ago, who started and won the fight for free, public, and universal education as the gateway to equality and the good life! The thought of Harvard's quarter-million for writing may reawaken a little hope that in one place at least literacy has a fair chance to stage a comeback. But let us be practical: if you had this sum in hand, how would you begin?

9

Confronting Crisis

I know the answer that would come from a good many quarters: make a study — find out what's wrong with our teaching in the grades — develop more modern methods — be "innovative" — that's the great word, never mind what it means. When the last of the $250,000 has gone down the gullet of a greedy computer, all will be well. The study will be reviewed in the professional journals. It will be called "on the whole, impressive . . . ." It will show that "in 92% of the writing programs investigated, five of the 'projective factors' proved not weak, silly, stupid, useless, but 'substandard'." The five failing factors proved to be only these: grammar, vocabulary, syntax, punctuation, and spelling. The rest — that is to say, paper and pencil — were adequate. Handwriting, with a "projective factor" of plus or minus five, just got by. Then six months after the publication of the study, a late reviewer will point out that the "statistical method used by the investigators is open to serious objections." Nobody will say one word about how well or how badly the study is written, which might be revealing. Who, indeed, could tell, among those who deal in this kind of literature?

I offer this bit of imaginary history to make emphatic my view of the state of writing today. The bad state of writing, the state of bad writing, is not due solely to bad teaching. The bad teaching itself is due to many influences that prevent good writing, that interfere with the clear thought inseparable from good writing. In other words, the writing done or not done today is a product of ideas and attitudes that pervade society and is not merely a product of the school world; it is a cultural and not simply an educational failure.

Since this is so, it follows that unsatisfactory writing will not change when a supposed technical difficulty is removed by better methods, more money, and a new dean. Inability to write is the manifest embodiment of errors in our minds — errors about politics and morals, intellect and art, social relations, and, finally, education itself. I cannot hope in the time at my disposal to go into all the superstitions and thought-clichés which I see as affecting our behavior so adversely that our writing *necessarily* comes out obscure, incoherent, non-communicative, indefensible. I can only present a sampling of the deviations from sense that create the predicament we are discussing.

10

The first such deviation is illustrated by my little fairy tale of the new-born study and how it grew up to be innovative. Owing to the prestige of science, technology, and statistics, our first response to a predicament is: let's go at it indirectly, looking first at what is, and without any thought of what we want. Think of the Berkeley instructors *asking* if we still need to write. Nearly everybody I have talked to recently about writing has automatically assumed that nothing is known about the way to teach it right; has assumed that it was *methods* that must be wrong; has assumed that there must be a method to be found — a sort of pill, a pro-ceptive pill, which can be administered. In short, by the scientific twist of our minds we see *problems* where reality presents *difficulties*. Problems imply solutions. But in certain parts of life there are no solutions, only difficulties — which nothing will abolish. It will always be hard to write well and always hard to help another to write passably.

Accordingly, the prerequisites for a teacher are to know good writing when he or she sees it, and also to write acceptably. He or she need not master any new abstract method, but must practice writing and make the pupil practice, under a sensible mixture of criticism and encouragement. In freshman composition during the last fifty years, we have seen all the indirect methods fail, one after another: imitating models, doing pseudo-research, starting with a smattering of formal logic, summoning spontaneity by ignoring grammar and idiom. All these were evasions of the requirement that writing be done under the guidance of someone who can show how words work and why it matters to put them together right.

But do teachers generally know good writing at sight? Professor Joseph Williams of the English Department at the University of Chicago went around the high schools of his city — it was a study, if you like, a study in disillusion; for he found that school teachers preferred passages of abstract and clotted jargon to simple sentences that might contain one or two awkward turns. They passed the former with good grades and flunked the latter. We find here another cultural trait, now dominant all over the globe except perhaps in some blessedly backward spot: everybody talks abstract, pseudo-technical, would-be scientific language, because everybody reads and hears nothing else. If teachers prefer this language — in fact they know no other — pupils of course try to follow suit. And it is a language that cannot be taught right, being the enemy of clear thought to start with. Here is the outcome from the pen of a freshman at one of the best state universities in the country (Illinois):

"Of all the intelligent people I had the opportunity to meet, can be classified into three distinct types. The first of these is a person with a high intelligence toward academic studies, but has no cognition of current affairs. The second type also possess a knowledge of academic studies, but unlike the first, he has a fair acquaintance with current events. The third classification is a person who possess an outstanding knowledge of academic subjects and also is well acquainted with current happenings."

This young man is obviously no fool and he obviously can't write. He has been linguistically crippled on his way to college. For he cannot give clarity and force to the sensible idea that people should combine practical, contemporary knowledge with theoretical and historical. In eighty-three words he stumbles eight times, and in such a way as to show that he is incapable of straight thinking: he has no grasp of singular and plural; of the relation between a type or classification and a single member of that class; of the logic in prepositions that link ideas; and of the different applications of such words as *knowledge, intelligence,* and *cognition.* He is a highbrow in vocabulary and wishfulness and a retarded child in thought processes. In many ways he is a typical adult of today.

It is no defense of him or ourselves to say that one does manage to extract an idea from his illiterate paragraph, any more than it is an excuse of the status quo to say that when critics complain of bad writing they are looking for brilliant writing — the work of gifted craftsmen, masters of style. Qualified critics want nothing more than ordinary prose that can be read and understood at one sitting, instead of a sentence such as this from the Transportation Department in Washington: "This is to advise you in accordance with our external audit policy that we do not have requests for the audit of final vouchers for which the audit report will not be issued within six months of the date of your request."

Intelligence and general ability have nothing to do with the case. Lack of the power to think in words and through words is the cause. So true is this that an observant academic man has coined the phrase "straight-A illiterate" to define the species. He asks the brilliant student to explain his own writing or his own opinion and is offered again the language of non-thought. I said the type was frequent among adults today. Here is a Houston principal addressing the parents in his district:

"Our school's cross-graded, multiethnic, individualized learning program is designed to enhance the concept of an open-ended learning program with emphasis on a continuum of mul-tiethnic, academically enriched learning using the identified intellectually gifted child as the agent or director of his own learning."

What strikes the eye and the ear in this pseudo-language is that form, construction, articulation — in a word, grammar — play no part in it. This is not surprising, since the teaching of grammar has been largely given up. Most of you know why this has happened. In reviewing the causes, we encounter again the influence of science, but soon discover it in alliance with a strong social and political animus — all of these, let me repeat, attitudes and ideas prevailing in the world at large and not confined to the world of schools.

The scientific impetus that destroyed the teaching of grammar came through modern linguistics. In its attempt to become a science, linguistics preached the doctrine of "Hands off the language!" The old grammar prescribed this or that form. The new must only describe, which means taking down what anybody says just as he says it. As one linguist put it some years ago, "A native speaker cannot make a mistake." This is all very fine for the linguist — his sport is as engrossing as bird-watching. But it is useless for the teacher and for anybody who wants to write, because teaching and writing involve making practical decisions — using words this way or that, not both ways or ten different ways.

It is just at this point that the political ideas I spoke of, ideas of democracy and elitism, of individual rights and equality came in to strengthen the hand of the linguist and deal the death blow to any practical grammar, one that prescribes, which is to say *in-*

13

structs. The approved teaching became write, speak as you please. You have a scientific *and* democratic right to do so. Imposing a standard grammar is a form of oppression. The mother tongue belongs to all equally. The idea of correctness is elitist; self-expression knows no rules, for each self is unique.

These propositions were not really ideas; they were thought-clichés, and not any less effective for co-existing with their opposites. For example, if language is whatever anybody happens to say, what becomes of its power to communicate? If anything goes and words have no fixed meaning, why do dictionaries keep appearing? Again, if there are no grammatical norms, why do the linguists speak of standard English and sub-standard? "Correct" may be a dirty word and "standard" a scientific one, but surely "*sub*standard" is elitist — who is to say that somebody's speech is *sub* somebody else's?

Still more questionable is the practice of those same linguists in their talk and their books: all use standard English words arranged in grammatical ways, not very elegant perhaps, but ways that one would swear didn't deviate from correctness. Theory and practice are at odds here, and one gains the conviction that the democratic, egalitarian free-for-all preached in the books is really a terrible condescension: "*We* speak and write *well*, but we give you fellows permission to speak and write *good* — after all, you can't help it. You were born to uneducated parents or brought up in a dialect." The vogue of so-called Black English among educators a while ago was a demonstration of the same false democracy, actually a form of intolerable patronizing. Fortunately, black leaders saw through the unconscious snobbery and kept demanding that schools give all children as good a command of the standard tongue as possible. Any hope of social equality and democratic manners depends upon it. Think back again to the Berkeley investigation — do we need to teach the young to write? And consider that President Carter gets a ten-page report daily on the contents of seventy newspapers and magazines. Why not expect that a boy from Berkeley might some day want the job of writing that report?

But the harm has been done. Grammar no longer rules. Absurd attempts are made to teach the science of linguistics in junior high school by such devices as asking the pupils to compile a dictionary of local usage. Outside the schools, among adults, the same dogmatism has implanted similar superstitions, such as that language must be allowed to "live" and "grow" freely. Therefore never object to any form of words, never correct your children at home, and — by extension — never think twice about your own manhandling of grammar and idiom.

The linguist's laisser-faire chimed in with yet another general article of faith, the belief that all change is good. Change is inevitable, change is the sign of life; a changing language shows how lively it is. To interfere would stop progress. So once again, anything goes and the chances of decent writing — the counterpart of decent speech — are by so much reduced.

I trust that in this gathering I need not spell out the fallacies in the clichés I have just recited. It is enough to point out that it is not language that lives, but only those who speak it; and if they want to communicate efficiently they had better keep as clear and fixed as possible the symbols they use. We do not see physicists and chemists changing the meaning of their terms in order to have a more lively time and make the science "grow." And precisely because mankind's concerns are more numerous and complex and passionate than those of any science, it is desirable to save whole the inventions called words by which we can think and talk about these concerns.

But in spite of this simple common sense — if you have a code, keep it straight — it is evident from our modern behavior that strong impulses are at work in the other direction. To name them is to pass from social, political, and scientific notions to moral and artistic ones. We had the spectacle, less than ten years ago, of students all over the world proclaiming their right to what they called "free speech," by which they meant a steady stream of obscenities. It is instructive to reflect on that outburst as an intellectual and moral phenomenon. The words liberated in free speech were those formerly excluded from ordinary conversation, and up to that time the restraint was by common consent. Nobody could possibly enforce it, so the revolt was not especially heroic. As to the words themselves, they were few and not particularly expressive, which means that in use they had to be repeated so often that they soon lost both meaning and the

15

power to shock — rapidly diminishing returns for so violent an effort.

One can see, however, that on the principle of "anything goes" which had prevailed for a couple of generations and which declared any forms of speech acceptable, it was logical to let the dirty words have currency also. They were the last ones still under wraps — at least among what used to be called decent people. But we should remember that those words had entered literature — the most advanced literature — since the heyday of the naturalistic novel; and remember also that the incessant use of those words accompanied the fighting of two world wars. From the trenches and the foxholes, the words came back with redoubled energy to the highbrow stage and the slim volumes of existentialist and other poetry. And there these met another powerful linguistic tendency, likewise emancipated. From Rimbaud to Yeats and from Joyce to Ionesco, one finds precedent for every species of obscurity, of grammar flouted, syntax destroyed, and words twisted or recast into unrecognizable shapes.

It would be foolish to underestimate the effect and spread of this literary current. The man in the street may never have heard of *Finnegan's Wake*, but he treats words with a deliberate freedom never heard before. Advertising has helped to instil this permissiveness, and its effect differs radically from that of the earnest mistakes by which in earlier ages languages changed. Until this century both educated and uneducated speakers felt that the forms of words must be rigidly observed if one was not to be thought ignorant and ridiculous. Now playing with language is the mark of the self-protecting mind. How did this reversal come about?

I think we can attribute it to the feeling of oppression and regimentation produced by the modern world. Never mind whether the feeling is justified or not, the sensation is that of being hemmed in, pushed about, controlled by outside forces, and this breeds an impatient hostility to rules and forms that breaks out in periodic *cultural* revolts. The earliest of these was the artistic one I just mentioned and the latest, beginning with student "free speech," is all about us. It is permanent revolt. I recently read an interview with a well-known, middle-aged French novelist who is no radical. It ended with a few questions about his favorite books, pastimes, and so on, including: "What sort of people do you like best?" His answer was: "Those who disobey."

In that pervasive mood of the times, it is clearly difficult to teach the forms and rules of writing. The student — it has happened to me — will invoke the example of the great artist. "If Joyce can scramble words, why can't I?" And the reply can no longer be authoritative, let alone authoritarian. For the teacher, like the reader of books or spectator of plays, is now face to face with a new kind of self-conscious self. The tacit understanding of former times that the student does as he is asked and that the artist works to please his audience — that implied contract no longer holds. The broken contract, the disobedience admired by the French novelist, signify not only an escape from surrounding oppression, but also a boost to the self-regard, the ego, which modern man has been taught to nurse. I mean quite literally taught. Indiscriminate permissiveness, the slogans of self-expression and self-development, the parents' fear of their children, the abolition of homework, the discrediting of manners, the premium put on originality, the overgrown elective system, the granting of privileges and rewards without requiring them to be earned, the prejudice against correction and reproof, coupled with the suppression of failure, the use of bribes for performance, and the non-enforcement of stated penalties — all these messages of love on easy terms have bred a twentieth-century character which some captious critics would prefer to call a non-character.

I say non-character, because, though we might find some children of grace who would thrive by being given perpetually free choice, most children are children of the law, who lose by having no law. Brought up as they are, they cannot be blamed for confusing self-development with taking the path of least resistance; they naturally mistake conceited ignorance for originality; and they learn the habit of disobeying, because they have been told that the self is a precious piece of china to be protected from every pressure. And, too often, it turns out that this self is a mere hypothesis; it is actually non-existent, and we then have the anxious searching for a self — the identity crisis — which might not have occurred if the self had been given a chance to *make* itself (it can't be *found* like a lost umbrella), the making of a self being possible only through alternate bouts of response to demand and the free exercise of new powers.

In this view, the state of writing today reflects the absence not alone of trained ability, but also the absence of character. A sidelight is thrown on this likelihood by a recent letter from an earnest teacher to the *Times* of London. She reports her conversation with a high school girl, whose interest in lucidity she was trying to arouse: "But Sue, if you were writing to your boyfriend, you'd want him to understand the letter." "What would I want to write to him for?" "Well, suppose he went away to another job?" "If he went away, I'd get me a new boyfriend."

On this side of the ocean, here is an illustration of the pervasive self-indulgence shown through its unexpected opposite. The Katherine Gibbs school trains secretaries. In a feature story about it, the *New York Times* tells us that a young woman there, after making a series of typing mistakes, was "suddenly ashamed . . . , yanked the paper from her machine and inserted a fresh sheet. She knew she would lose a minute from her typing exercise, but it would not do to hand that sheet in. Not at Katie Gibbs!" The incident plainly says: everywhere else, sloppiness and inaccuracy are accepted routine. Somehow, Katie Gibbs can make a young woman "suddenly ashamed." Moral character matters at least in one small oasis.

But by and large the principle is in abeyance, as we find, for instance, in the educational innovation reported from Louisville, Kentucky, where last November, the Free Public Library offered a hamburger to every child who registered for a card and took out a book. Juvenile registration increased by 34.5% during the first month. The library has been eagerly scanning circulation figures ever since to see if the increase is proportional to the weight of hamburger consumed.

The foregoing facts and comments are enough, I am sure, to spur your memory and imagination and persuade you, out of your own experience, that the present state of writing has not come about as the result solely of bad or mistaken teaching. Bad writing today is the offprint of our prevailing state of mind, a true expression of contemporary thought and feeling, the outcome of what we do and *prefer* in all the important fields of human action, from science and social relations to private morality and highbrow art. Until we think and feel differently, we shall only tinker uselessly, and neither writing nor the teaching of writing will improve. Despite statistical studies and innovations, the freshman I quoted will not in four years of college be remedialized — or if you prefer, remediated. The social and intellectual menace he represents will not be *remedied* until he perceives that clear writing is a civil duty matching his civil rights, a part of the social contract that guarantees his own protection and privileges. And he cannot be expected to see this connection until the world around him understands it also.

But the goal of my discussion being practical, I want shortly to return to the scene where education and pedagogy supposedly mesh but actually fight each other. They do so, because — once again — the surrounding culture lacks an understanding of both. But before I am ready to take you back to the schoolroom, I must remind you of a few more obstacles to reform and hindrances to good writing.

Some of you may expect that I am going to mention television. If so, you are wrong. The news, sporting events, and especially commercials exert on the whole a very good influence on speech *and* writing, since many of these features are written first, and they are clear because written to be read. Much more harmful are the program guests who come from academic life, the other professions, and the world of art. These people have acquired the worst faults of democratic-industrial speech — jargon, abstraction, vague metaphor, and atrophy of thought. I call it democratic and not *popular* speech, because now as in the past it is a democratic trait to inflate utterance, to talk highfalutin, and go in for pretentiousness and pedantry. Look up James Russell Lowell's Preface to the second *Bigelow Papers*, dated 1869 — over a century ago — and you will see what I mean.

In language, the democratic impulse is to dignify and cover up. The plain names of ordinary objects are too common and there is, very often, a touching but mistaken desire to avoid hurting others' feelings. For example, old people are called senior citizens. It is a foolish, self-defeating ploy, because at every use, the senior citizen — such as myself — is reminded that he is old and that it is so dreadful to be old that he has to be called something else. Similarly, the poor, the lame, the backward nations, the sick, the blind, the mad, the stupid, the criminal have all been rebaptized, sugar-coated for general acceptance. I have just come across the name of a worthy school where people who stutter go in hopes of being cured. It is called The Precision Fluency Shaping Program. That unutterable, unstutterable phrase is another sign of our enfeebled character; at the same time it shows the democratic urge to glamorize by loose, inaccurate terms vaguely suggestive of science. I invite you to pursue this notion further by looking behind the acronyms that pockmark our prose like measles: most of the names of the organizations sporting four or five initials are disgraceful exaggerations of simple purposes.

In all these too is an urge to separate words from things, to leave no stone naked but to dress it up in artificial moss. Let me give you a small example. It used to be that when one wanted a telephone number not in the book, one would dial *Information.* Though abstract and four syllables long, the term was still too simple and direct. Some itchy executive at Bell Telephone resolved and campaigned to rename it Directory Assistance. What's wrong with that? Everything. To begin with, it is twice as long, to say and to print. In the second place, it destroys any idea relevant to the subject. You want information; you do not want directory assistance, for you have a directory and it doesn't assist you. Nor is it that you need assistance in the use of your directory: you know the alphabet already. What is more, no foreigner knowing English can guess what the words mean. What then would be the plain, self-explaining, popular but non-*democratized* way of calling that necessary service? It stares you in the face, provided you have not entirely lost the feel for things, acts, persons, desires. The name of the service should simply be "Number, please." But I wager that if the change were proposed, hundreds of objections would defeat it — because it goes against the current. Study the frequent re-namings of groups, departments, and the like — they are all patterned after the endless tapeworm and are indestructible, short of killing the body it lives in.

20

It is no wonder that the educational system has been powerless against so many outside forces, largely unconscious and therefore totally uncontrolled. To teach clarity, order, simplicity, or even spelling in the emotional and intellectual anarchy of modern utterance is an heroic task performed by only a few maniacal dissenters here and there across the country. The rest are either defeated, defeatists, or delegates of public opinion, who reinforce it by passing it on to the young.

What is more, inspired by these attitudes and emotions endemic in society, teachers and administrators have built systems and followed practices which virtually guarantee that good writing and its essence, straight thinking, are not taught. At the source, teachers' colleges wallow in "methods," which are for the most part pretentious platitudes couched in woolly prose. The study of subjects — as against methods — is rarely encouraged. Clearly, it is more difficult than "methods," even when it is not sharper in thought and expression. The new names of subjects — language arts, instead of English; social studies instead of history and civics — display the familiar desire to blur the contour of reality, and hence to make thinking and writing painfully hard. Read James Koerner on the preparation of our teachers.

Consider next the universal use of workbooks and objective tests, both based on the practice of hurling the mind at some short challenge in order to choose a prepared answer and put a mark in the little square box. This act, a million times repeated, is a true symbol of our illiteracy. In the old days, those who could not write would make an X and a clerk would write below, "Peter, his mark." In an objective test, the pupil never has to summon up his own words to frame an answer, never has to sift his ideas to improve the phrasing of that answer. In place of such positive exertions, he need only catch the drift of someone else's wording two or three times and reject it. What is left is the so-called answer.

To be sure, some people have felt qualms about this perfect conditioning against the act of writing, and in response the College Entrance Examination Board reintroduced an essay question in its tests. Then the Board took it out again, then put it back. Now you see it, now you don't. But the shilly-shallying was sensible enough. How can decent essays be written by youngsters who have not been shown how, who have not been drilled in the details of form in their school years, and who — instead — have sailed through a dozen subjects by putting "Peter, his mark" in the right hand margin of innumerable printed sheets? The sudden essay question "late in life" — as you might say — is monstrously unfair.

If anyone doubts that the prevailing temper of the school is dead set against the *principles* of good writing, one only has to listen to some of the persistent clichés teachers and principals repeat: "You don't need to learn to write well — if you get on in the world you can always hire a secretary." Where she (or he) will learn is not stated. Or again: "Good writing is too complicated and subtle for the modern generation to learn." Presumably, medicine, physics, and the law are not complicated and subtle — modern youth finds them a perfect cinch. Still more unjust to youth is the assumption that "background" permits or prevents the learning of such rudiments as reading and writing — as if this country had not been peopled and developed by millions whose ancestors did *not* read and write. The fact is, reading and writing themselves were *invented by illiterates* — and since that time every person of normal mind can be brought to share that heritage.

But the spirit of mechanization in schoolteaching defeats the possibility. It is background that decides; it is objective tests that tell us who is best; it is classroom methods that work, or some innovation, based on taking down partitions or on wall-to-wall carpeting, that is going to remove all difficulties. One looks in vain for a human mind and the recognition that there is no substitute for direct effort long drawn out.

The pursuit of labor-saving has given us the teaching machine, which now gathers dust in numberless storerooms, and more recently the absurd attempt at computer-grading for actual written work. The proposal shows how hopeless it is to expect good writing from our schools except by accident, when the school philosophers can entertain such an idea as computer grading. This is it: statistical analysis showed that grading by computer closely matched grading by four different readers — human readers. Therefore the computer was as good as they. But how did the computer grade? Again by statistical analysis, a correlation was found between a high grade and the following features — the length of the essay, the length of the words used, the average deviation in length of words, and the number of marks of punctuation, especially commas. Success seemed assured until somebody pointed out that a haphazard jumbling of the words and the putting down of a dozen commas all close together at one end would give the product a grade equal to that of the original readable essay.

In colleges, where anger and invective about bad writing are always aimed at the schools, the practices are futile and unjust in other ways. The English department is expected, all by itself, to produce good writing. No instructor in any other subject bothers to correct any written work or any spoken answer. "I teach chemistry, not English." The message is plain: only English teachers have to be placated by readable stuff — or by the pretense of caring about what's being said.

Freshman English is the one and only writing course required — hence it is a bore, a term in jail, an outrage. The teaching is assigned to the most junior staff members. Most of them have never taught, they have rarely thought about writing, about words, have never read a book on the subject. Few can write well themselves or know that they don't. If they are given good-sized classes at the same time as they struggle toward a degree, the course is equally hated by teacher and taught. And knowing all this, the great scholars who sit above the treadmill feel nothing but contempt for it. It is on a par with cleaning latrines in the army — and far less effective.

In short, from kindergarten to Ph.D., the system works against the attainment of articulate expression. Everybody pays lip service to it without demanding it or imparting it. Good writing is very nice when you can get it, it comes like a fair summer day, but when serious people discuss serious things, writing comes after a host of other wants.

This generality is what makes the present outcries so remarkable. Instead of the usual complaint from the same old grumblers, we are now hearing from people who sound as if in sudden pain. The Chief Justice of the Supreme Court recently broke precedent by calling down counsel for writing a brief 216 pages long. The case did not justify the length, which resulted from verbal incompetence. On the West Coast, a lawyer is in court maintaining that the income tax statute is unconstitutional because it cannot be understood. In the Department of Health, Education, and Welfare, a group of civil servants assigned to draft regulations — about health, education, and welfare — have been told to take a course in English composition, because the drafts they sent up to the Secretary were unfathomable. And as you may remember, in his first fireside chat, President Carter promised us simplified statements of government rules.

He was promising the millennium. The day after this rash undertaking, a former legal adviser to the government declared that of twelve hundred regulations issued yearly about consumer products, "no one in the White House or Cabinet can understand any, and there is hardly a person in Washington who can completely understand even two of them." But this expensive lunacy is beginning to bother at least some officials, however used to it they may be. The Secretary of Agriculture has told his department that he will not sign a directive he cannot understand. That is a revolutionary move — it makes one think of heroes like Patrick Henry, Luther, Joan of Arc; imagine *refusing* to sign something you can't understand!

To be sure, another Washington official softened the blow by explaining that "few Government employees are trained to write regulations." He could have excused the government entirely had he said that few people are trained to write, few of any sort, age, or occupation, including professional writers — as any publisher could testify. There was a time, in the bad old days, when the ambition to serve one's fellowman as doctor, lawyer, scholar, journalist, clergyman implied without question that one had mastered the ancillary art of writing, because the necessity for it was clear to all. That is what we have lost through softening of the brain and character. And we shall not recover in the least degree the ability to write clearly for the public and professions until that necessity is felt once again. All the fireside chats and Cabinet gestures will accomplish nothing.

Am I then telling you that we are in the hopeless condition predicted in the story of the Tower of Babel? No. What I am saying is, on the one hand, that Babel is near — not yet built, but

Jacques Barzun

we're digging the hole for it very fast; and I am saying on the other hand that unless we know why we need clear words to achieve whatever we want to do, we shall not be able to restore the simple, obvious discipline by which good writing can be taught.

Let me conclude briefly with the practical reasons and suggestions I promised on our subject: What is the universal necessity for decent writing? First, *to increase accuracy.* Misunderstanding is easy and natural; carrying the right idea out of one skull into another is hard and unnatural. Second, *to economize attention.* All of us suffer from the bombardment of stimuli and the shortness of time. The Chief Justice said that if every night the bench must read a brief of 216 pages, the work of the Court would so pile up as to defeat justice altogether. Third, *to clarify individual opinion.* Anyone who writes even passably well knows what he thinks far better than one who does not write or writes badly. The act of writing is a task of *sorting out,* which helps to eliminate foolishness, prejudice, inconsistency, and dull clichés. Fourth, *to speed up action.* This hardly needs comment after what officials tell us about their own rules and what citizens endure as a result. All of us are perpetually filling out forms or trying to follow written directions. Each such operation takes twice or three times as long as it should on account of bad writing. Fifth, *to see through fraud, deceit, propaganda.* Whoever writes well has learned to scan words for meanings hidden and overt and will automatically detect the rhetorical tricks by which irrelevancies and gaps in logic are concealed or made plausible. Sixth, *to extend and make more subtle the enjoyment from human communication.* There is no need to argue for what is as great a pleasure as music or painting. But why do I list it under necessity? Simply because without more pleasure of the sort that words afford we stand a good chance, not of building Babel, but much sooner of going down a steep place like the Gadarene swine.

The necessity of good writing once established and felt, how do we go about teaching good writing — teaching it early and late, so that it becomes habitual and yields the pleasure and profit just cited? Supposing the cultural blocks removed — a big supposition — the task is absurdly simple:

Confronting Crisis

1. *Good writing* has two prerequisites: frequent writing and invariable *rewriting*. As in all other arts, regular practice is indispensable and as in some other arts, repeated self-correction, the struggle to perfect some one piece of work, is the only path to even modest accomplishment. Merely reading critical comments in the margins of a bad paper does nothing for the paper or the writer.

2. *Good writing* presupposes reading good prose, continually, as well as reading aloud and speaking extempore under teacher supervision and class criticism. Good prose, in the sense here intended, means classical prose rather than contemporary, for the reasons stated earlier.

3. *Good writing* cannot be taught directly: the pupil teaches himself, under prodding and encouragement from a teacher who knows what good prose is and can write it too. The teacher's awareness of the pupil's difficulties must include a knowledge of what themes and what degree of mastery are appropriate at each stage of development, which faults are grievous and which are venial, what merits are most praiseworthy, and how individual talents vary in the amount and kind of work they are able to produce. The teacher of writing, in short, must know how to teach *writing*.

4. Therefore the training of teachers must match that of the school children and college students: What do teachers read? How do they write? Who coaches and corrects their writing and how? Teachers' colleges take notice.

5. The textbooks and workbooks and "objective" tests used in school and in teachers' colleges are due for re-examination in the light of these criteria. Much of what is written and circulated among teachers must be eliminated as poisoning the very source of verbal expression. The common medium exchange in a school or college should show the same qualities as those desired in the writing of the student and the graduate. Any contradiction here is both absurd and destructive of the professed aim.

6. Arguments against discipline in writing are also absurd. Spontaneity, free inspiration, self-expression are qualities much to be desired, but they do not survive lack of technique.

As you see, the prescription is not complicated or abstruse. It does not even taste bitter, being but the coordinated acts of reading and uttering intelligently. Yet for the time being there are in this country — at a rough guess — some two hundred million reasons against following the prescription and getting cured.

William A. Owens, born in Blossom, Texas, November 2, 1905, was educated formally at Southern Methodist University, Dallas, and at State University, Iowa. Informally, he received his education in the cotton fields and among the folk of East Texas. His career as professor of creative writing has taken him back and forth from Texas universities to Columbia. His reputation as collector of folk literature and folk music is rivaled only by his creative works based on his own experiences, as *This Stubborn Soil* and *Fair and Happy Land*.

William A. Owens

To Make Literature of Our Lives

For most of my life I have been concerned with learning how to write, writing, and teaching others the mechanics of writing — long enough to know that of all taskmasters writing is one of the most demanding, and one of the most difficult to reduce to principles. It is then with suggestions and not with formulas that I speak, not with arrogance but with humility. Anyone who has taught five sections of freshman composition in one semester will know the humility I feel.

I speak also with what I take as a specific charge from the editors: to discuss "the value of experience as the subject of writing — not just narrating it but analyzing and evaluating it. Too often our students have been asked to write about literature instead of making literature of our lives." Keeping that charge in mind, I feel free to keep my own personal experience near the center as I discuss both writing and the teaching of writing. Jacques Barzun has given a pessimistic view of what we have lost in writing skills. I share that pessimism. At the same time I am optimistic that the general outcry against growing illiteracy will compel us to insist on standards of excellence for some, competency for all.

29

Confronting Crisis

I am convinced that, though writing as an art cannot be taught, the essential mechanics can be, and that most students can be guided into satisfactory use of the written language, if their teachers are willing to spend the necessary time, energy, and patience — if they are willing to forego their own pleasure in emoting on the sonnets of Elizabeth Barrett Browning or in explicating word by word, line by line a poem like "Sunday Morning" by Wallace Stevens. These pleasures, as I will explain later on, have their place — in literature but not in composition classes.

As a student I was fortunate enough to have more than my share of good teachers of composition. With a certain pleasure in sounding old-fashioned, even old-fogyish, I will recite what some of them did for me.

The first was Tyler Frank Jessee, my teacher in the sixth grade at Pin Hook, down by the Red River in Texas. To him a noun was a noun and not to be confused with any other part of speech, and next to the word in importance was the sentence. He had a hundred sentences that we parsed and then diagrammed until I could recite all their parts without looking at the blackboard. Years later, when my publishers asked me to get a release from him for certain passages in *This Stubborn Soil*, he read slowly, quietly, and then looked up with satisfaction on his face. "I always did say I could teach grammar," he said. He could. Even now, when I write a sentence that seems shaky I take time to diagram it before I let it stand. Lately, to my embarrassment, I let a sentence with unpardonable syntax get by. An editor marked it and wrote in the margin: "This sentence don't work." That editor was Jacques Barzun.

Ruth Hudson, my teacher in freshman composition, kept the emphasis on grammar and at the same time led the class into the study of models for writing. Her method was to have us memorize, not poetry but prose. Concerned with both form and substance, she elected the personal essay as the form and Robert Louis Stevenson as our model. Week in, week out, we memorized passages, almost with the same respect we had when we memorized passages from the King James version in Sunday School. On both depth and beauty Stevenson came out second, but still with enough impression on me for me to be able to close my eyes and see that classroom as I repeat, "Laziness is a quality for cattle," and the antithesis, "Extreme busyness is a sign of deficient mentality." For longer assignments she sent me to autobiographical books, among them *Far Away And Long Ago* and *The Purple Land*, both by W. H. Hudson, who remains one of my models to this day.

A third teacher to whom I owe more than I can say was Henry Nash Smith. His was my first class devoted largely to writing. He was my first teacher who was himself a writer. His concentration was on the word, first as image and then as symbol, and after that on legend, myth, and ritual. Mr. Jessee and Miss Hudson were pre-Freudian. Henry Smith was definitely post-Freudian. In class he spent little time on Freud and his works but enough for us to understand his liberating influence on writing. Almost as if for my special benefit he required extensive reading in Sir James Frazer's *The Golden Bough*. Thus he provided means for me to explore my folk language and ways and to write about things I drew from folk memory. Unfortunately, while he was beginning to liberate me he was liberating himself out of a job. He was fired for writing the preface to William Faulkner's *Miss Zilphia Gant*, which some of his superiors found obscene and sacrilegious.

These things were done for me, and I am grateful. I should like to spend a few minutes on what was done to me, especially in some of the literature courses required of me in the Ph.D. program. I refer to what I call the process of reshaping a person into an academic. The process was systematic and sterile as far as my development as a writer was concerned, not because of the literature I read but because of criticisms of literature I was forced to absorb and repeat. The Ph.D. as I experienced it seemed designed to eradicate from the language any spontaneity or any relation to life itself, and to substitute jargon for the Anglo-Saxon flavored language I had grown up with. At times I lent myself willingly to the process, with disastrous results in my writing. I wrote *zounds* when I meant *God damn it* and thought myself clever. In an early draft of what became *Look To The River* I had the boy crossing the greensward when I really meant that he was crossing a Texas cow pasture. Made ashamed of my East Texas uncouthness, I turned to nineteenth-century

31

bookishness. I know that as a writer taking the Ph.D. was the worst thing I could have done. I know also that, having taken it, the best thing I did was to enlist in the army as a buck private. It took less than three weeks for the corporals and privates and a bastard top sergeant to knock the academic out of me.

I am not here to argue against the Ph.D. I do feel that in the typical Ph.D. program the emphasis is on literature rather than writing, to such an extent that teaching composition is regarded as an inferior occupation and young teachers are encouraged to escape composition courses as soon as they can. Where the college is part of a graduate system the composition courses are too frequently assigned to graduate students. No matter how dedicated they are to teaching, they are students first, teachers second. They must devote their energies to graduate study, and they are less experienced in the classroom. They simply are not well enough prepared to combat the errors of poor or misguided teaching in high school composition classes.

Lately, as a member of a community committee studying the English curriculum in the Nyack, New York, High School, I have been able to learn why Johnny can't write. Too many teachers of high school English are themselves unable to write. They find teaching composition infinitely boring and turn to filling class hours with interminable discussions, sometimes of literature, often of social and political problems. They invade the territory of social science teachers, who also may not be able to write or to guide their students in writing. For standard courses they have substituted film making and media (television) criticism, but no basket weaving. They profess to be in search of something called relevancy. Students are bombarded daily with relevancy, a word they make sound synonymous with escapism. Two other words are of prime importance in their lexicon: interaction and inter-relatedness. The latter is defined in the Nyack High School syllabus as follows: "This term is used throughout to refer to the inter-relatedness of the student/teacher as a unit."

Those curriculum builders included a statement that unwittingly gets at the heart of one problem:

William A. Owens

Loss of interest is a definite biproduct of a student's not getting individual attention, but more than that, is the repetition of undetected errors and perpetualization of poor learning further compounded if material is not spot checked and progress is not charted.

Dig that word *perpetualization*.

Here we have defined a chain of errors that has been going on half a century or more — too long. Students, in English as well as in the other disciplines, leave graduate school poorly trained in writing. They inflict their errors on their students. Worse, not knowing better, they legitimize the errors with praise and high grades. Furthermore, no good teacher of writing ever "spot checked" a student's paper. Thus what they call "perpetualization of poor learning" is their link in a chain not easily broken.

At the risk of belaboring the problem too much, I should like to read from the same syllabus the introduction to a course called "An Approach to Corrective/Developmental Writing":

Since the nature of writing problems surfacing in writing electives vary with each student, originating from a broad base of experience, individual attention is indicated as a first step toward solution. It would be well to note that even the most articulate student has room for growth in written expression. Therefore, the following is recommended (with an awareness of time and space constraints) not only as a help for the student with severe problems, but as an opportunity to expand the capabilities of students with an abundance of talent.

Unfortunately this statement takes no note of teachers who themselves have serious problems in writing — teachers who are holding onto some kind of educational jargon and perpetuating their own bad training.

As I see it, teaching of composition in high school has been captured by the jargon makers, the self-styled activists, and the would-be literary elitists. Instead of sending students to a library to read a book they send them to a "learning resources center" to view a film of the book or to do "in-depth research" on a subject as remote as the social problems of aborigines in the Northwest Territory of Australia. Such assignments can easily

33

Confronting Crisis

lead to non-writing, especially in classes in which students "interrelate" with the teacher and each other in oral rather than written "critiques." Students are allowed to develop their arguments into shouting matches, but they are not required to reduce them to written words. Teachers, pleading a heavy burden of work, are willing to substitute short-answer, easily graded tests for essays of any length. It should not be surprising that high schools graduate students unable to read job applications, recipes, or their own diplomas.

We have been in this particular chain of being long enough for this trained incompetence to have penetrated our universities to the highest levels, with even more disastrous results. Sadly, college students find the teaching in writing little improved over that in high school. Many colleges, yielding to the trend, no longer offer composition courses. Many composition courses that remain are turned into anything but the hard discipline of writing, correcting, rewriting — activities that require hard work and long hours for teachers and students. The loss in man hours through incompetent writing is incalculable. Consider the conscientious director of doctoral dissertations who works and works with a student to make his composition acceptable and ends up rewriting large sections himself. Consider how much damage one such Ph.D. can inflict during his academic career.

I feel that all teachers should be required to pass a writing test before appointment, as I feel that all high school students should pass a writing test before diplomas can be granted. To break the chain that has us bound, I would recommend that these tests be graded by persons who can prove that they have not absorbed the jargon that now displaces clear, concise language. Furthermore, I believe that all teachers of English should be teachers of composition.

Too often I hear teachers complain that their students can't write because they don't have anything to write about. Their solution is to assign them a topic in literature — one of their own or one selected from a published list of topics for research papers. Often the topic is so unfamiliar that the student is forced to consult summaries and commentaries. If the student is a poor reader as well as a poor writer the whole assignment from initial outline to completed paper is an exercise in futility.

34

William A. Owens

The study of literature has its rewards for the writer as well as for the critic and the general reader, if the piece is read in its entirety and perceived as a direct communication one mind to another. Adaptations and condensations abound. I know a man who owns a copy of every *Reader's Digest* condensed book ever published. So do critics and interpreters. The student must be warned that the study of someone else's study of literature can become stultifying. He must be made aware that literature is the recreation of personal experience, personal emotion, and that true relevancy comes in the recognition that something he has experienced in literature illuminates and lifts his own spirit. I should like to illustrate with two incidents from my army career.

In the first I was at Camp Ritchie in Western Maryland, training in both counter and combat intelligence. On an April morning we were up at four and on a hike that would take us twelve miles up hill, down hill, and across narrow valleys. Dawn came when we were working our way through a dark hemlock forest. The sun rose when we were at the top of a hill and going into double time for the sharp descent. As we came around a bend I saw something I had never seen before, a cherry orchard in full bloom. Suddenly words were surging through my mind:

> Loveliest of trees, the cherry now
> Is hung with bloom along the bough,
> And stands about the woodland ride
> Wearing white for Eastertide.

In the cadence of "hup, tup, thrip, four" there was no time for lingering, or in the corporal's yelling, "Shag your butt, grandma." Never mind. In one glance I had enough understanding of the poet's understanding to sustain me the whole day.

The other incident was on the beach the second night after the Leyte landing. I had the midnight watch outside our headquarters, with death so close that I was ordered to cover the radium dial of my watch, cock my carbine without a click, and tread noiselessly in my jungle boots. Japanese soldiers were within yards of us, unseen, trigger happy. Silently I paced back and forth in the ghostly whiteness of a bomber's moon. Unconsciously and then consciously I was seeing the ghost scene from Hamlet, seeing it, feeling it, shivering from the fear that permeates it, shivering from fear of an enemy crouching close,

35

waiting. As if impelled I began the great soliloquy, the words formed but not sounded. Not all of it would come but the irony for me was clear: "To be, or not to be: that is the question." The choice was not mine to make. It might be made by a Japanese sniper walking a post close enough to see me as a shadow. Time passed and there was a friendly touch on my shoulder. My relief had come. My watch had ended. Gratefully I felt my way back to my cot, but not to sleep. Relief had come but not release. I still had to live with a heightened sense of fear.

The war over, my very soul staggered by too much of death and destruction, I came home determined to grab people by any hold I could and make them see and feel the sights and sounds of war. My problem was that I was forty years old and still did not know how to write. On what seemed a long chance I registered for writing courses at Columbia University and whacked at the typewriter as many hours a day as I could.

The next semester I was asked to teach the courses I was taking, courses called writing, not composition. Never before had I been given so much freedom in a classroom, so much freedom and so much responsibility. My colleagues set no rules, assigned no task other than to teach. My classes were filled with young men, most of them ex-service men, who said: "I have come here to learn how to write. Please show me how." They had their own stories of the war to tell. They were demanding, and frank. The question came not to me but to one of my colleagues: "What right have you to teach writing? You have never published anything."

Though I had published a little, I took his question to heart. For nearly three years I studied what others had to say on writing and passed on to my students any techniques I gleaned. At the same time I applied what I had learned to the novel I was working on, *Walking On Borrowed Land*. I took it as a compliment when my agent, after reading the manuscript, said of me: "He has learned everything that he has taught his students."

Through many misdirections I learned that writing class is not a literature class. Readings, when they are undertaken, must be more for technique than for meaning, no matter how important the meaning. Writing must be the major activity — writing, correcting, rewriting, even to the point of rubbing off the early bloom of the piece. Few of my students come prepared to write. They come with a vague yearning to write, or with the mistaken belief that writing is an easy way to make a living, that writing is as easy as talking. Too many of them have not learned simplest mechanics of punctuation, sentence structure, paragraphing. Smugly they argue that they will depend on a secretary or an editor to clean up their mistakes in spelling and punctuation. They have to learn the hard way that secretaries are no better trained than they are, and that editing is costly — so costly that manuscripts requiring extensive work are likely to be turned down.

Writing students come to class with great enthusiasm and premature questions on how to get an agent or how to copyright their material. Inevitably they learn that they are not ready for either. The dilettante drops out quickly. The most serious become tardy in handing in manuscripts, tardy in reading the work of their fellow students. For me, student writing must be the basis for class meeting. The teacher cannot fall back on discussions of literature. No manuscript, no class must be his policy. Only on one occasion have my students failed me completely. There was not one page of new writing. In my frustration I grabbed the Manhattan telephone directory and took it to class. It fell open at the *m*'s and I began reading in my usual flat voice name, address, telephone number. The students looked at me and at each other, but did not stop me. I finished one column and was well into the next when a young man raised his hand. "Yes?" I asked. "Too many characters, not enough plot." When the laughter subsided I set them to writing stories about one character selected from the telephone directory. Teaching writing is not like any other teaching.

Through both teaching and writing I have become convinced that the writer's own experience is his most valid resource. What better does a person know than the regions of his own mind? The beginning writer can draw from his own mind the sense of immediacy and authenticity. He does not have to struggle with acquired impressions and acquired technique at the same time. As he matures in his craft he learns that incidents in his life can be added to, taken from, distorted to arrive at truth, at universality.

37

Confronting Crisis

Perhaps I can better illustrate with my first novel, *Walking On Borrowed Land*, published in 1954. It grew not from a single irritant but from an accumulation of observations of ill-treatment of blacks. Through boyhood and young manhood I accepted without question the white attitudes endemic in East Texas and most of the South, attitudes of condescension and disrespect, attitudes that led to subtle and overt cruelty. As a mature man I began the study of Negro music, both sacred and secular, a study that took me into churches and homes and honkytonks. I saw their side of the tracks, with the poverty, violence, waste — always the waste of human energy, of potential talent. The facts of discrimination became painfully clear. The need to dramatize them and arrive at some moral statement about them became equally clear. I set out to dramatize the facts of waste — waste of talent, waste of humanness one to the other, waste of life itself. My voice was the voice of Mose Ingram, a teacher like me. I need not review his story here. I will read a summation of the conviction I arrived at, as it appears in Mose's final words:

> "My people are a happy people, a talented people, a religious people," he said to himself in the darkness. "They have the strength of great faith, the weakness of deep superstition. They have come a long way since the days of slavery. They have the will to move ahead. God grant me the strength to go with them."

I am not saying that the writer should restrict himself to personal experience. Eventually interest or self-interest will impel him to make a region unknown as familiar in his mind as the long-known. Wittingly he will so deeply absorb other times, other places that they will be as fast fixed in his memory as anything he has known or done. What I regret is that teachers, instead of asking students to look into themselves and write, assign topics so foreign that energy is used up in research and there is none left to expend on the writing. The result is half-baked at best.

Self-knowledge is hard to come by. The spark that would inflame the imagination may be easily overlooked. An incident with the greatest initial impact may be the most difficult to analyze, and in the end unsuited for writing. A detail barely noticed at the time of happening may be the fact that triggers moral and ethical speculation. In *A Season Of Weathering* the facts of circumstance destroyed the tranquility of a Sunday morning walk:

> I found myself looking back over four generations of life in Pin Hook. I was the fifth. No one remembered how it came to be called Pin Hook, but the name had been known a long time, perhaps for nearly a century — or why. Perhaps as a joke on a place at the back end of nowhere. In a hundred years life had changed little — for many not at all. The life cycle might still be as short as forty years: birth, marriage, death, the years between filled with a little schooling, much hard work on worn-out land, begetting of children who would begin the cycle all over again.
>
> The day was, I realized, another journey in search of myself, of trying to find out what spark from what generation had sent me away from Pin Hook, what spark had brought me back, what spark made me content to be back. If not a spark, then a chemistry of the soil? I could see the boys and girls in my grades following the life cycles of their parents, too many hookworm kids begetting too many hookworm kids. In me the cycle had been broken, by what I did not know.

For a closing I turn again to that Robert Louis Stevenson I knew so long ago. He wrote, "Man is a creature who lives not upon bread alone but principally by catch words." No doubt he had his list of catch words. We certainly have our own. How will we ever break the chain, loosen their grip? The answer lies in the will of English teachers wherever they are to accept nothing but the best. Otherwise, critics can justifiably say that English is too precious to be left in the hands of English teachers.

Richard Benson Sewall was born in Albany, New York, February 11, 1908. He received his Ph.D. degree from Yale and, after a year's service at Clark University, he returned to Yale where he remained to distinguish himself as an eminent authority on the life and poetry of Emily Dickinson. "Why not a book called *Teachers in America*?" he has asked. "I remember being inspired by Jacques Barzun's *Teacher in America* during my early years as a teacher."

Richard B. Sewall

Working Words

This paper will be "simple, sensuous, passionate." It concerns "Working Words" and points directly to students. I want it to suggest certain questions: How much of the wonderful stuff we teach — which, after all, is simply words put together most remarkably by gifted men and women — how much of it works? How much of it enters alive into the minds and hearts of our students to bring about a change? How much of it sticks? I want my readers to be haunted, plagued, dogged by these questions. For, unless some of what we teach, in some way or other, at some time or other, actually works, we are wasting our time. In the words of the locker room, we'd better hang up our spiked shoes.

That's the "simple" part of my paper — a tiny jeremiad, as you see. Nothing new, simply true. Now for the "sensuous" and "passionate" part — the way, of course, literature works. I shall proceed by examples.

Let me start with a reference to an article about a Shakespeare course for non-English majors at Western Carolina University. The article, by Professor James Nicholl, concerned a student of Mr. Nicholl's, a most unlikely candidate for such a course — a business major, a married man, an Army veteran interested, it seemed, as much in his motorcycle as in his studies,

41

silent in class, apparently not with it at all. After the course was over and the marks in, he paid a surprise visit to Mr. Nicholl's office. After all the silence, he had something to say. It turned out to be about *Othello*. "You know," he said, "the ending of *Othello*, with him killing Desdemona and all, you know, it's kind of sad." Here, from what had seemed pure stone, had come a drop of heart's blood. Mr. Nicholl made this comment: "I was impressed . . . that this particular student, a groundling if there ever was one, had admitted that the play had affected him; he had been touched, had felt 'sympathy,' had been humanized, if only a little." Or to put it in the terms of this speech, the words had worked.

Here's another story. Again it's a steal, this time from a satirical review that toured the country about fifteen years ago called *The Second City*, an American version of the British review, *Beyond the Fringe*. (The second city, of course, was Chicago.) One skit I remember in detail, though I may be off on some of the particulars. A father enters the room of his sixteen-year-old daughter, who is reading a book by a famous psychologist. She is annoyed at being interrupted, but Father zeros in regardless. "Helen, I want to talk to you — seriously. Your mother and I want to know what went on at Freddie Smithers' party last Saturday night." Helen is hostile and evasive; but finally, after much prodding, the truth comes out: "We experimented." Father's temperature rises: "And what did you experiment with, pray tell?" "Well, if you want to know, we smoked dope." (Fifteen years ago that was a much more horrendous matter than it is now; the audience, I remember, gasped.) Father blew his top. He spluttered on about the police and the family honor and the danger of drugs. Helen was unmoved, aloof, distant. Finally, seeing that he was getting nowhere, Father changed his tactic. His voice softened. "Helen," he asked, "are you in love with Freddie Smithers?" Helen stiffened. "Dad, I don't know what you mean by love. It's loving, Dad." And she held up the book she'd been reading, Erich Fromm's *The Art of Loving*. "Dad," she said condescendingly, "I'm afraid you and I are not talking on the same level of discourse." But Father — a very perceptive father — had seen his opening. "Helen," he asked, "have you ever read *Romeo and Juliet*?" "Yes," she

mumbled, "last year in school." "Helen, do you remember when
Juliet is talking to herself about Romeo and how much she loves
him, and how she longs for him, and how she can't wait for night
to come so she can see him again? Do you remember what she
says?" Then, with infinite tenderness, Father recites those
marvelous lines. Somewhere Father had taken a course in
Shakespeare, and it had stuck. The words had worked. And now
he makes them work for Helen.

> Come, night! come, Romeo! come, thou day in night!
> For thou wilt lie upon the wings of night
> Whiter than new snow upon a raven's back.
> Come, gentle night; come, loving, black-brow'd night;
> Give me my Romeo; and, when he shall die,
> Take him and cut him out in little stars,
> And he will make the face of heaven so fine
> That all the world will be in love with night
> And pay no worship to the garish sun.
> O, I have bought the mansion of a love,
> But not possess'd it; and though I am sold,
> Not yet enjoy'd. So tedious is this day
> As is the night before some festival
> To an impatient child that hath new robes
> And may not wear them.

By this time, Helen is in tears. The hostility, the distance, the
"levels of discourse," the finicky distinction between "love" and
"loving" are all gone. She is a girl in love, and she is in despair.
With her head on her father's shoulder, she sobs, "Yes, Dad, I
love Freddie — but he doesn't care for me." The curtain slowly
lowers to the sound of Helen's sobs and her father's consoling
murmurs.

Like the young motorcyclist, Helen had been "touched,"
she had been humanized, she had joined the human race. The
words had worked.

Another example, this one from my experience teaching in
the Navy V-12 program during the war. We'd been using a little
book of selections, *Thought in English Prose*, edited by an
English schoolmaster, J. C. Dent, published in this country in
1930. (It has often been imitated but never excelled.) One of the
selections was Dr. Johnson's *Preface to the Dictionary*, about as
unlikely a piece as one can imagine to throw at a bunch of gobs,

all in uniform, and some of them veterans of the South Pacific campaign. After the discussion had covered the rhetorical and structural questions Mr. Dent had set us, I found myself reading to the class the passage in the *Preface* where Dr. Johnson in his bitterness describes the long ordeal, now at last ended, of composing the *Dictionary*; how he had worked "with little assistance of the learned, and without any patronage of the great; not in the soft obscurities of retirement, or under the shelter of academic bowers, but amid inconvenience and distraction, in sickness and in sorrow. . . ." Then he concludes: "I have protracted my work till most of those whom I wished to please have sunk into the grave, and success and miscarriage are empty sounds; I therefore dismiss it with frigid tranquility, having little to fear or hope from censure or from praise." Perhaps I read the last sentence with heightened feeling. I'd just been fired from Yale, and I could understand Dr. Johnson's bitterness and frustration. At any rate, one of the boys stopped after class with a strange look in his eye. "That was terrific," he said. "What was?" I asked. "That 'frigid tranquility' stuff." "Sure, it's good," I said, "but what's so terrific about it?" Then he explained in short, sharp Brooklynese: "I was on the beach at Iwo Jima, see? We won, all right. But what did I see all around me? My buddies all shot to hell. I was lucky. Hadn't a scratch. But what did I do? Did I shout and cheer? Hell no. I looked around me and what did I feel? That guy was right: frigid tranquility."

I've thought about that incident a good deal. It says a lot about the miracle of words. Dr. Johnson on the beach at Iwo!

Professor Donald Sears of the University of California at Fullerton has reported the surprising success of a required course in Milton, a cause he had considered all but lost. To test what he thought was the waning interest in Milton on his campus, he added a question to his final exam: "What in Milton seems to you most vital and valuable to a twentieth-century reader?" Mr. Sears quotes many of the answers, some of them eloquent and perceptive and almost all of them positive, pro-Milton. This was "very heart-warming," he writes, "to an aging Miltonist." Summing up the answers, he describes their pervasive theme: ". . . the simple, transporting beauty of the words. It is perhaps in a moment of appreciation and wonder . . . that we become most human, most divine." Nothing could better describe what I'm trying to bring into focus: those tiny but redeeming epiphanies when words miraculously work.

No one was more sensitive to the transporting power of words than Emily Dickinson. "In the beginning was the Word" has been well said of her. She was in awe of words. She wrote to her friend Joseph Lyman:

> We used to think, Joseph, when I was an unsifted girl [she borrowed the adjective from *Hamlet*] and you so scholarly that words were cheap & weak. Now I don't know of anything so mighty. There are [those] to which I lift my hat when I see them sitting princelike among their peers on the page. Sometimes I write one, and look at his outlines till he glows as no sapphire.

Words, she knew, could wound — "She dealt her pretty words like Blades" — and they could kill: "Infection in the sentence breeds." But mostly they were life-giving, restorative. "You need the balsam word," she wrote her bereaved cousins. "At every word I read I seemed to feel new strength," she wrote a friend when she was ill. And there's her poem:

> He ate and drank the precious Words —
> His Spirit grew robust —
> He knew no more that he was poor,
> Nor that his frame was Dust —
> He danced along the dingy Days
> And this Bequest of Wings
> Was but a Book — What Liberty
> A loosened spirit brings —

To get back to the students: I don't picture any of them exactly "dancing along the dingy Days" after a required course in Milton, and I don't suppose our young Shakespearean gave up his motorcycle for *Othello*. One in a thousand, perhaps fewer, will respond to a book in Emily Dickinson's total way. But you can't tell. If our motorcyclists and our Navy gobs and our Helens don't actually "eat and drink the precious words," they know for a redeeming moment their transporting power.

And now comes the question: How can we as teachers bring about this effect more often? What do we do? Sometimes it's just luck. When I was beginning to teach, one of the older men in our department said: "You can talk yourself blue in the face all term and get nowhere. Then an adjective you drop on the street-corner makes over a student's life." Surely I had no idea that the phrase "frigid tranquility" would so reach that Navy boy. Rule Number 1, perhaps, is that you have to "feel it" yourself, if only a little bit. I don't mean that you have to be in love to teach Juliet's great speech to "black-brow'd night" — but it helps; at the very least you'd better know a little something about what being in love feels like. And when you come to Dr. Johnson, it's not a bad idea to have felt a little of that "frigid tranquility" in your own blood stream. In short, if we're going to be humanists, we'd better be human — and as honest and as articulate and as generous in sharing our humanity as we can possibly be.

Thinking back over my own experience, mostly as a student, several other suggestions come to mind. I think we should read aloud as much as the traffic will bear, and as persuasively as possible. I hardly remember a word of what many of my teachers said, but I remember what they read. One miraculous day in the Old English course in the graduate school — by its nature a gruelling, disciplinary affair — the teacher left the minutiae of grammar and syntax for a moment of pure transport. We'd been slugging through that passage where life is compared, in its fleetingness, to a bird flying into a crowded banquet hall and out through a window on the opposite side. Our instructor was moved to a moment of reflection and unprecedented self-revelation. He looked out the window and quoted, from memory, Swinburne's despairing lines:

> From too much love of living,
> From hope and fear set free,
> We thank with brief thanks-giving
> Whatever gods may be
> That no life lives forever;
> That dead men rise up never;
> That even the weariest river
> Winds somewhere safe to sea.

"I don't agree with that," he said. "I don't believe it — but there are moments in my life when it helps." I learned more about lyric poetry and its uses from that than from whole books of learned analysis. The comment was powerful, but it was the reading that really worked.

46

Richard B. Sewall

Again: a crowded lecture hall, with the great William Lyon Phelps regaling us on modern poetry. Mostly, I'm sorry to report, inanities. Then in the question period, a great moment. "What do you think of A. E. Housman?" someone asked Billy; and with perfect aplomb he stepped to the edge of the platform and recited, beautifully, the famous poem:

> Loveliest of trees, the cherry now
> Is hung with bloom along the bough,
> And stands about the woodland ride
> Wearing white for Eastertide.
>
> Now, of my threescore years and ten,
> Twenty will not come again,
> And take from seventy springs a score,
> It only leaves me fifty more.
>
> And since to look at things in bloom
> Fifty springs are little room,
> About the woodlands I will go
> To see the cherry hung with snow.

Billy didn't miss a beat. No pauses, no stumbling. Five hundred people held their breaths. It was unforgettable. "That's what I think of Housman," said Billy.

There's a passage in *The Way of All Flesh* that I'll paraphrase. Young Ernest Pontifex is having trouble with his studies — a hard passage in Milton, say. He goes to his Aunt Aletha for help. She reads the passage to him, aloud, slowly. "Do you understand it now?" she asks. "Oh, yes," answers Ernest, "I understand it when you read it."

Another suggestion: it should be clear by now that I believe in memorizing, in getting students to beat into their heads as much as they can hold: short lyrics, certainly, or the first eighteen lines of the *Prologue to The Canterbury Tales* or the opening passage of *Paradise Lost*. Sometimes the words will work in no other way; that is, make sense, full sense, play on the young pulses and in the young blood streams. Coming back to Chaucer recently after a twenty year lay off, I wondered if the current crop would willingly submit to the ancient assignment of learning the eighteen lines from the *Prologue*. I got them to listen to the recorded readings available in the audio center, and I listened to each student recite the lines in my office. It worked. The

47

sound, the rhythm, the full sense hit them all at once and all together. Many of them said it was the best thing they'd done so far in their education. The words had come alive.

> A Word made Flesh is seldom
> And tremblingly partook
> Nor then perhaps reported —
> But, have I not mistook,
> Each one of us has tasted
> With ecstasies of stealth
> The very food debated
> To our specific strength —
>
> A Word that breathes distinctly
> Has not the power to die
> Cohesive as the Spirit
> It may expire if He —
> "Made Flesh and dwelt among us"
> Could condescension be! —
> Like this consent of Language,
> This loved Philology.

If it's the function of the poet, or the dramatist, or the novelist, to bring about the "consent of language" Emily Dickinson is talking about, then it's our function as teachers to make the poem, or play, or novel live and breathe for our students. For our motorcyclist, Desdemona for a moment lived, and her death was sad. For Helen, Juliet, in the rapture and impatience of her love, lived, and that sophisticated young lady was reduced to tears. Dr. Johnson's honest rendering of his own experience helped clarify the experience of a young man two hundred years later. Chaucer's words, Milton's words, still work — if we will only let them.

It's one thing to inform our students. We do that daily, and should. The mechanics of language; techniques of reading and writing; facts, methods, theories — all these are necessary and good in their own way. But it's another thing to transform them. That's our ultimate mission, the ideal we strive for. I've tried to show how, perhaps, it's more within our reach than, in moments of discouragement, we think. It can be done. It has been done. Now — and here's the pastoral charge — let's do it.

Charles Leland Sonnichsen, native son of Iowa and adopted son of the Southwest, was born September 20, 1901. Educated at the University of Minnesota and Harvard, he taught at the St. James School in Minnesota and Carnegie Institute of Technology before establishing himself at the University of Texas at El Paso. There he ran the spectrum of academe from professorship to chairmanship to deanship, publishing prolifically in Western history and culture. Sonnichsen lives at present in Tucson, Arizona, where he is editor and director of publications for the Arizona Historical Society.

C. L. Sonnichsen

The Folklore of Academe

A century and a half ago, Emerson delivered his Phi Beta Kappa address, *The American Scholar*, in which he defined the scholar as "Man Thinking" and advised him to be "free and brave. Free even to the definition of freedom, 'without any hindrance that does not arise out of his own constitution.' " Ever since then the American college professor, who is or tries to be the American scholar, has suffered from delusions of grandeur.

Strangely enough the American taxpayer, who provides the professor's salary, has been slow to ask if he is getting his money's worth. He has tended to take the professor at his own valuation, regarding him as something not to be tampered with, called to account, or handled roughly. Who wants to disturb Man Thinking?

There are signs that the tide has turned. In some states the taxpayers are finding out that the latest models have no brakes or mufflers and ought to be sent back to the factory. Most of our fellow citizens, however, tend to find something mystical in the Ph.D. and to think of the scholar as somehow set apart.

I agree wholeheartedly that scholars, who are mostly professors, are a separate breed of men. I have lived among them for over fifty years. I know as much about them as anybody needs to know. As one of Dickens' characters says, "*I* know their tricks

51

and their manners!" I am not, I hasten to add, violently anti-professor. Some of them are my best friends. I don't think, I must admit, that I would want my daughter to marry one, and if I had to be cast ashore on a desert island, and were looking for a suitable person to be cast away with, it would not be a professor. But I look on scholarly types with more amazement than hostility, and one reason for my amazement is the transformation they have undergone during the half century I have had them under observation.

When I first became aware of them, a scholar was somebody who read books and taught young people for a living. He admired the classics. He loved words and ideas. He wrote a little — a textbook or two; a novel that nobody read; nothing that could tax his energies or destroy his peace of mind. He wore clothes that had been out of style for years and he looked a little rumpled. Everybody thought he was odd but almost everybody loved him. He was, in short, a gentleman and a scholar.

When I was in graduate school, I used to hear about Dean Briggs of Harvard, long since retired but still a semi-sacred memory. Although he lived well into the age of automobiles, he used to drive his horse and buggy down to his place on Cape Cod every summer. Behind his house in Cambridge he had a small orchard which he cared for himself. One day he put on his rustiest old clothes and climbed up into one of his fruit trees with a pair of pruning shears. His neighbor, an aggressive New England matron, looked over the fence and addressed him with natural condescension: "My good man, when you finish with that tree, will you come over and trim mine?" Dean Briggs said, "Certainly, Ma'am," and did so without argument or explanation. He was a scholar and a gentleman.

I used to know Professor J. B. Wharey of the University of Texas, a well-known Bunyan scholar who came to the campus in the early years of the century when Texas was considered to be the world's largest cow pasture, inhabited almost exclusively by cowboys. He was still teaching when I spent a semester there as a visiting professor in the middle thirties. He and Mrs. Wharey attended a lecture and song recital by Carl Sandburg one night in the course of which Mr. Sandburg gave a spirited rendition of "The Ballad of Sam Hall." When he came to the lines "My name

it is Sam Hall, and I hate you one and all! I hate you one and all,
God damn your eyes!" Dr. and Mrs. Wharey rose with some os-
tentation and walked out of the hall. Dr. Wharey was, according
to the standards of those days, a gentleman and a scholar.

I never became well acquainted with Professor Morgan Calloway of The English Department at The University of Texas,
but I saw him sometimes and knew about his work on the Anglo-
Saxon infinitive. He wrote a monograph on it, which was
recognized by specialists in early English as the authoritative
work in this area. Anyone with a deep yearning to learn about
the Anglo-Saxon infinitive inevitably found himself in the arms
of Calloway. Naturally there were skeptics. To J. Frank Dobie,
who snorted at all "academicians," Dr. Calloway was the
epitome of scholarly futility and his work was the best justifica-
tion of the view that scholarship consists in taking unimportant
facts from one inaccessible place and putting them in another.
When Dr. Calloway died, according to campus legend, a colleague met Mr. Dobie and asked if he intended to go to the
funeral. "No," Mr. Dobie replied, "but I approve."

The halls and offices of learning used to be full of Briggses
and Whareys and Calloways. I could describe fifty more of them,
and so could any man who has spent his life in the precincts and
purlieus of scholarship. They all had the courage of their ec-
centricities. They were all built pretty much to Emerson's
specifications and tried to act like Man Thinking — in-
dependently. At the same time they were mindful of the rights
and needs of others, labored hard in their vocations, and were
treated with deep respect enlivened by amusement.

Since those days a new breed has arisen, and it scares me. If
I had to give a brief definition of the modern scholar, I would
say: "A scholar is a university professor who can qualify for a
grant." If I were allowed more words, I would define him as "A
specialist who publishes articles that nobody wants to read on
subjects that nobody is curious about — and wants to teach his
specialty no more than six hours a week to four graduate students for $40,000 for nine months, with allowance for a research
assistant and for travel."

Next to his passion for research and publication, his major
ambition is to keep lesser scholars off the graduate faculty (he in-

Confronting Crisis

sists that they must publish ten articles in top scholarly journals, or one book and five articles, before they are fit company for him). His favorite indoor sport is getting on programs of professional societies as critic or respondent and roughing up the rising young scholar who leaves his rear uncovered. He is keen on distinction, promotion, top salary, and a minimum teaching load. He is a bit of a savage, and I would call him a Buccaneer of Academe. He has not been riding quite as high since the oversupply of Ph.D.s hit us in 1970, but he is still very much with us.

Sometimes his native ferocity is increased by a revolutionary bias. He believes that capitalism is effete and vicious, the American middle class is materialistic and corrupt, social justice is impossible to attain by peaceful means, and the campus is the proper arena for fighting the minions of corruption and greed. Often he advertises his position by wearing working men's clothes and growing as much hair as he can. He scorns conventional morals, thinks that obscene language makes things real, and is open minded (wide open) about sex, drugs and campus violence.

I have watched these new-model scholars arrive and go into action on my campus. You have watched them on yours. They seem to me a symptom of something that goes much deeper than fads in teaching techniques or hair styles. They are the result of the revolution in education which is going on from the kindergarten to the graduate school — probably part of an even greater *malaise* over Things As They Are.

The theorists in the realm of childhood education tell us that the old ways of teaching and learning are inefficient and even injurious to the child. What we need, they say, first of all are open classrooms without assignments, homework, examinations or grades — friendly little clubs where the child chooses what he wants to learn and often learns it by acting it out, getting rid in the process of pent-up hostilities, frustrations and death wishes. The new university scholars likewise reject the old ways of teaching and learning. The idea is to get the student involved, shock him out of his lethargy and indifference (the product of years of classroom boredom), and make sure his eyes are open even if he remains illiterate. To work from a syllabus or call a class roll would be an unthinkable concession to mouldy tradi-

54

C. L. Sonnichsen

tion. They bring coffee cups to class, take off their shoes, and lit-
ter the floors with cigarette butts. They want everything to be
free and natural, motivated by student interest. A lecture is the
ultimate abomination, and some of them won't even start a discussion — refuse to open their mouths until a student brings up a
discussable question. There is a feeling that if a young person
knows he is learning something, he will be turned off at once.

A multitude of experimenters and analysts are hammering
away at the problem from every point of view. They agree on
only one thing: the traditional approaches are vicious and must
be got rid of. So much has been written that nobody could ever
read it all, but the general direction is clear. It is summed up in
Deschooling Society, by Ivan Illich, described as "a powerful
argument that 'for most men the right to learn is curtailed by the
obligation to attend school.' "

We hear it every day. In fact, we hear nothing else. If
anybody attempted to defend the American system of education,
on any level, nobody would listen to him, nobody would publish
him, nobody would believe him. A Ph.D. dissertation submitted
by Michael Sexton at the University of Iowa in 1972 describes,
with photographic illustrations, the plight of the schools:
"They're depersonalizing pupils and teachers alike. . . . I've tried
to show all the problems, frustrations, long hours and disappointments."

Well, what is wrong with having a few problems, frustrations, long hours and disappointments? Is there any human activity without them, including farming and the automobile
business and marriage? The best lessons we ever learn come from
our problems, frustrations, long hours and disappointments. Of
course the schools could be improved. All human beings and all
their endeavors need improvement. Why these people expect the
classroom to be Utopia is the real problem. But they do indeed
expect it, and they believe that unless we get rid of all traditional
patterns and start over — right now — we are facing ruin. The
shock wave is felt throughout the system and there is as much
uneasiness and dread in the university as there is anywhere. The
traditionalists are afraid the worst will happen. The
revolutionists are afraid it won't happen. The men caught in the
middle try to be confident that it may all be for the best and that

55

Confronting Crisis

the turmoil will eventually produce some sort of equilibrium.

The prevailing confusion accounts for some puzzling aspects of scholarship and scholars in our time, but not all. And this brings me back to my title. Outsiders with a fresh point of view can sometimes see deeper into a problem than insiders. An anthropologist opens up new insights for a psychologist. I suggest that a folklorist can understand the scholarly mind better than a scholar can.

Rightly viewed, folklore is the most important influence in our lives. It includes, according to one definition, "traditional beliefs, legends, sayings, customs, etc., preserved unreflectively among a people." The important word is *unreflectively*. Much of what we do and believe and say is done and believed and said because we do and believe and say it. We assume that our assumptions are right and true, and we tend to live by them. They are our private folklore. They include our prejudices and our ideals. We do not examine them or reflect on them, and we would rather die than give them up.

We stand in the midst of illustrations. Look at the buttons on your coat sleeve. When gentlemen buttoned back their cuffs, those buttons served a purpose. The purpose no longer exists, but could you persuade a tailor to make you a coat without buttons on the sleeve? No, you couldn't. Coats always have buttons on sleeves. If you want to be eccentric, you can go to another tailor.

I once heard a formula for telling where a man is from. You call him a liar and watch what happens. If he is from Texas, he stabs you or shoots you, or at least knocks you down. If he is from up around Ohio, he looks you in the eye and says firmly, "You're another!" If he is from New Hampshire, he puts a spear of timothy in his mouth, chews for a moment, and replies, "Well, you can't prove it."

In short, we do what is expected of us and assume that it is right, or at least necessary. This is true of all groups of people: children, politicians, businessmen, and scholars — especially scholars.

I find that they operate from two basic assumptions. The first of these involves RESPONSIBILITY; the second is a matter of FUNCTION.

C. L. Sonnichsen

In the area of responsibility, it seems to me that most scholars have ceased to think rationally at all. All of us, even scholars, know that freedom is relative — that everybody is responsible to somebody. In practice university scholars refuse to admit any such thing. They cling to Emerson's idea that the scholar should be "without any hindrance that does not arise out of his own constitution." They are not even responsible to God. They don't believe in HIM any more. The key phrase is ACADEMIC FREEDOM, which means that no controls are acceptable.

Two groups especially must keep hands off: the taxpayers and the university administrators. Any attempt by either of them to exert influence affects a scholar as the senior Hamlet's ghost affected the watchers on the platform at Elsinore Castle. His hair rises "like quills upon the fretful porpentine."

Some years ago I was a member of a search committee looking for a new president. The rumor that the townspeople were in favor of this or that candidate raised the hackles of every member of the committee, except me. I felt that the people who were paying the bills had some rights too. But as a minority of one, I kept my thoughts to myself.

It is worse if the president or the dean takes a hand. Suppose an English teacher passes out a sexy poem or assigns the students theme topics defending free love or homosexuality. If the administration refuses to renew his contract, the academic community is up in arms, and if the administration refuses to be intimidated, a number of liberal professors, who would never distribute obscenities themselves, will resign and look for a place where the intellectual climate is freer.

Their conduct can be understood only if we remember their folklore — the assumptions they live by. One such assumption is that no interference with academic freedom is tolerable. They are inaccessible to reason on this subject. They think they are making a great sacrifice for a principle. And so they are. So is a Japanese who commits harakiri. Both are victims of their own folklore.

The second assumption a scholar lives by involves his function — what he is for. He will tell you that as a scholar he is deeply engaged in the search for truth. True, he makes his living

57

as a teacher but he does not particularly love teaching and does as little of it as he can. The only way scholars can gain recognition is through publication, and their only yardstick for measuring success is the length of a man's bibliography. If the bibliography is long enough and the man can prove thereby that he is a producing scholar, he gets his load reduced. In short, the best college teacher is the one who teaches least. By a simple extension of the principle, the very best is the one who does not teach at all.

If this principle were applied to motherhood, the best mother would be the one with the fewest children, and the best of all would be the woman with none. Into such absurdities a strict adherence to our folklore can lead us.

Research, as we all know, is the key word in the scholar's vocabulary. A scholarly person becomes so by the intelligent and thorough exploration of source material. Where does the source material come from? In most cases it comes from other people. In short, research is picking other people's brains. It could just as well be called scavenging, shoplifting, cannibalism, or just plain theft. The nice word for it is "documentation." This means that if you lift another man's thought or language, it is all right if you admit that you lifted it. This assumption is part of the folklore of scholarship.

The folklore in this case, as in many others, involves observing a set of rules. Almost all taboos can be broken if you follow the proper procedure. The Ten Commandments say, "Thou shalt not covet," but it is all right if you have a mortgage. Again, "Thou shalt not bear false witness" — but if you run an advertising agency, it is expected of you.

The business of productive scholarship has its rules likewise. I distinguish six of them:

1. THINK BIG. Respectability depends on the amount of brain picking you do. If you get all your information from one book, you are a plagiarist and can expect to be sued. If you use material from fifty books, you are a scholar. If you use material from a hundred, you are an authority. A parallel situation exists in the world of finance. If you can get away with a million dollars, you are a financier.

2. BE BOLD. This is where the documentation comes in. You admit in your notes that you got your material from somebody else. The more notes, the better the scholarship. Great scholars sometimes have more notes than text. Possibly the ideal situation would be all notes and no text at all.

3. BE CAUTIOUS. Remember that custom permits quotations of fifty words or less in reviews and scholarly works without asking permission of author or publisher, but if you put the ideas in your own words, you can claim them for your very own. You can be sued for verbal borrowings but almost never for borrowing ideas.

4. BE THOROUGH. The Supreme Sin is to overlook something. Other scholars are alert for any indication that you have missed a key source, and they will kill you if they catch you. A good thief gets it all.

5. REMEMBER WHERE YOU GOT IT. I once heard of a professor who got up his lectures and delivered them unchanged for years. He eventually came to believe that they had been given to him as the Ten Commandments were given to Moses. When he retired, he decided to put his material into a book and was immediately taken into court for plagiarism. This can happen to anybody who forgets that scholarship is picking other people's brains.

6. BE DULL. All scholars react violently against any lightness of touch, any use of the imagination, any play of fancy or wit. Scholarship, unless it is produced by a Frenchman or an Englishman, must be boring just as medicine must taste bad and virtue must be painful

It would be useless to deny that there is some overstatement in the foregoing paragraphs, but there is also much obvious truth. I look at the situation from this angle, however, only to make my point — that scholars live by assumptions which they seldom examine critically. If they did, they could not fail to see that there is an element of absurdity in what they live for and by.

If everybody lives by his assumptions, then I must admit that I live by mine. I grew up in the grip of what has been called the Puritan Ethic. I survived the Depression when the world did not owe anybody a living, or an education, and it was a privilege to have a job. I had to do all sorts of menial tasks to get through college, and I thought an education was priceless even though it was authoritarian, cognitive rather than affective, unconcerned about my emotional needs, based on lectures and textbook assignments and examinations, and oftentimes arduous, monotonous and painful to endure. As a result my mind is closed about certain things. I will always be immovably convinced that peace is better than war, that cleanliness is better than dirt, that hard work is better than idleness. I believe, and always will believe, that learning is better than ignorance. I am sure that learning is difficult and takes real effort, but I believe it is important and is worth drudging and suffering for. I believe that the wise should instruct the ignorant if they want to learn, and if they don't want to learn, they should go and do something else. My folklore tells me that it is better to repair than to destroy — that only an idiot burns down the house because he doesn't like the bathroom. My experience tells me that nobody is being discriminated against if he has a chance to better himself, even though he has to start at the bottom.

This makes me a conservative, a member of the establishment. I suppose I am a male chauvinist pig. Whatever I am, I have to think I am right because these attitudes are my basic assumptions, my folklore. I have to believe that my violent young friends will return to sanity — that is to say, to my set of assumptions. I am obliged to hope that the scholar and the gentleman, in some form, will return to us and be respected again. But I am realist enough, or folklorist enough, to be aware that if and when he reappears, it will be with a different set of assumptions and I may not recognize him or like him. That, however, is the way things work out in the most peculiar, if not the best, of all possible worlds. All any of us can do is to try to understand it a little better.

James Sledd, born December 5, 1914, in Atlanta, Georgia, was "the son and grandson on both sides of Methodist preachers." He "did" a B.A. at Emory and a second B.A. at Oxford as a Rhodes scholar. From there he went to the University of Texas, where he "did" his Ph.D. After teaching at the University of Chicago he won awards from the Ford, Rockefeller, and Guggenheim foundations and went to Chicago, Michigan, and Oxford again for post-doctoral work. Following duty at a number of "way-stations," he reached Austin again, where he has remained and in his words, has "perpetrated a few books and a lot of articles and reviews," and indulged himself in "an unchecked tendency to talk too much."

James Sledd

Can These Bones Live
—And Should They?

The bones I'm going to talk about are yours and mine — the old bones of a profession which has forgot to teach the people knowledge; and the answer to both my questions is: probably not. Dryden provides an epigraph less incongruous than the words of the Preacher:

> All, all of a piece throughout:
> Thy chase had a beast in view;
> Thy wars brought nothing about;
> Thy lovers were all untrue.
> 'Tis well an old age is out,
> And time to begin a new.

Maybe the last two verses are a bit optimistic.

Not to make things too hard on either of us as I play historian and prophet, I won't wash off the greasepaint or change the baggy trousers yet, and I'll limit the history to the last twenty years or so, which I began on the hills behind Berkeley, California, watching the dirty little reddish light of Sputnik-I as it cruised across a still-unpolluted sky.

In retrospect, my insensibility is obvious. Where I saw only a reddish light, more enterprising colleagues saw a path of gold,

63

and The Profession began the 1960s with committees and publications to prove that the national interest was identical with the prosperity of English teachers. Those were great days for manipulatory educationists. Terrified bureaucrats began to spend millions to overcome the Russians' apparent lead in filling the sky with radioactive junk, and colleges and universities began to double their enrollments of future intellectuals who would save virginal capitalism from the lustful embraces of godless communism. Real war in Viet Nam didn't bother anybody much at first. I know I never thought about it, though on the first day of 1960 I was in Asia, assigned to teach the children of Sinhalese peasants enough English in six months so that they could get a university education through English as a medium. I've since done even more foolish things — like trying to persuade my colleagues at UT Austin that it ought to be punishable to take the State's money for setting up phony courses.

Back in the States after my sojourn in Ceylon, and transported from the Pacific Coast to the Middle West, I engaged in ventures which made my Asiatic madness look like quintessential rationality. The federal government kept spewing money for education, and curriculum centers and summer institutes were springing up everywhere. As the middle-aged and ancient will recall, the idea was that college and university teachers would teach high school teachers and prepare curricula for them, so that high school students would be superlatively taught and would need no further elementary instruction when they entered the colleges and universities. Every crossroads college would then become a university, and every third-rate university would become "a graduate research institution of international reputation." I played the fool too, in my own small way. As an amateur of linguistics, I did my bit to damage some good high schools; but I strengthened my reputation for unamiable eccentricity when I opposed the establishment of a curriculum center at a university which had neither a plan for its operation nor personnel to staff it. With characteristic foresight, I moved to UT Austin to get away from academic politics.

H. L. Mencken once remarked that he was happy to live in the twentieth century in the United States of America, where never a day would pass without a good belly-laugh. By the time I went back to Austin (where I had earned my Ph.D. during World War II by bravely teaching air navigation aboard the *USS Garrison* — vulgarly known as Garrison Hall), by that time much of the money for research at the big universities was coming out of Washington; linguists at M.I.T. would soon be studying the meter of *Beowulf* at the expense of the U.S. Air Force; and the MLA was pushing the establishment of a National Foundation for the Humanities, so that professors who complained about their students' writing could be supported in comfort while they refused to teach their students how to write. My salary was paid last summer, and will be paid next summer, by the Endowment which that push begot.

But the vertical pronoun must vanish from these comments now. Wearisome clowning has no place in an eventual attempt at seriousness, and I mustn't suggest, by my manner of speaking, that I think what I have to say is more applicable to state universities in Texas than to state universities elsewhere. My examples may come from UT Austin, but that is only because I know it best. The argument depends, in fact, on the assumption that the big pattern-setting state universities are all basically alike, that they work together for common ends, and that indeed they are all built-in to the great interlocking national bureaucracy, where corporations and governments are hard to tell apart in their joint enterprise of subjecting the helpless many to the predatory few. The big state universities look less and less like educational institutions, more and more like research institutes; and their faculties are more and more concerned to consolidate their position of privilege and power as brains-for-sale to the whole vast machine.

In that great undertaking, the intellectual hired guns have enjoyed almost insuperable advantages. Ordinary Americans have had, and to some extent still have, an almost mystical reverence for booklearning; impressionable students can easily be persuaded to believe whatever enough professors tell them; and since most people haven't realized that higher education is no longer education but big business, and professors no longer teachers but entrepreneurs, the education lobby threatens to become as powerful as it is insatiate. In my view, among the

Confronting Crisis

greatest enemies of education in Texas is the Graduate Assembly
at UT Austin; and such once idealistic organizations as TACT
and the AAUP have made themselves comparable to the
Teamsters' Union and the highway lobby — front-organizations
for grossly selfish interest-groups. Only a catastrophe can stop
the mad research-machine, which is now running of its own
momentum beyond any rational control; but if the federal
government decides to buy its scientific and technological brains
elsewhere than on the campuses, the unbelievably extravagant
campus empires of the scientists and technologists will collapse,
though not before they have involved the rest of us in their finan-
cial ruin.

Many aspects of that thesis must be left undeveloped here,
notably the part which the universities played in the Viet Nam
debacle and the domestic disorders which accompanied it. Pon-
tification on those high and tragic matters would be contempt-
ible. My basic argument can after all be built within the petty
confines of one English teacher's vision and even with just one
course, the course in freshman composition, as the central object
of attention. Presumably not all of you would dismiss that
course as the graduate advisor in English at UT Austin did, a few
years ago, with the elegant and penetrating judgment, "Composition stinks."

Yet that graduate advisor's attitude has dominated The
Profession — dominated it to our loss. Unlike the scientists and
technologists, whose special skills can at least be made to appear
essential to government, industry, business, and the military,
professors of English have just one selling point that the tax-
paying public and its representatives may take seriously: we can
presumably help to cultivate general workaday literacy. But,
though we want to share power and privilege with the scientists
and technologists, we don't want to give the public what it pays
us for. We want instead to be paid, and paid richly, for doing
whatever we please — for inventing readings of Chaucer which
nobody else for six centuries has been fool enough to perpetrate,
for providing that iambic pentameter is not what the poets
who've used it have always thought it was, for neglecting the
study of our language but building a new fashion in criticism on
an outworn linguistic theory, and so on. The behavior of those

great men among us who pushed so hard for endowment for the humanities was typical. Knowing that Congress and citizens wanted literacy, our leaders dutifully complained that undergraduates can't write and that the graduate students whom we recruit to teach them are blind guides for the blind; but having uttered that ritual complaint, our humanists instantly denied its logical consequence, saying that if students haven't learned to write when they enter college, it's then too late to learn. Schoolteachers would have to do the work, but professors should get the money.

That kind of gross self-indulgence was not immediately disastrous in the fat 1960s. Enrollments were high and money plentiful, and many big universities put the humanists' no-principle into various practice. In 1967 at UT Austin, for example, the English Department launched a proposal to cut the composition requirement to just one semester, on the grounds that by 1968 two-thirds of the entering freshmen would write so well that they could be excused from the first course. There was no least evidence to support that claim. On the contrary, while the bureaucracy was announcing a two-thirds or even three-fourths exemption rate, the actual rate of earned exemption was less than twenty-five percent; but the ranked faculty of the English Department didn't want to be bothered about elementary teaching, because, as one much-praised assistant professor openly said, "We don't get raises or promotions for teaching freshmen."

Even such teaching of composition as did get done in the big state universities was thus assigned to armies of unprepared, overworked, underpaid teaching assistants, whose assistantships supported them, after a fashion, while they filled the professors' beloved seminars in a lemming-like migration toward Ph.D.s and permanent underemployment in the 1970s. Critics of the system were simply dismissed as soreheads, even by the TAs themselves, who recognized that an assistantship might not be much but was still better than nothing and who could not read the handwriting on the wall as the affluent bully-boy among the nations slipped from the summit of its power and began its long descent. Every graduate assistant imagined that some day he too would be a graduate professor, with his own retinue of slaveys —

and besides, with luck, a properly sycophantic assistant could get out of freshman composition and into sophomore literature. While the flush times lasted, the system was good for the ranked faculty, tolerable by the graduate students, and grossly damaging only to the freshmen and sophomores. Nobody cared about them in graduate research institutions of international reputation.

But the flush times didn't last. As the 1970s began, enrollment in the humanities was falling, money was tightening, and the job market for humanists had started to collapse. One would have thought that at this juncture, prudent academics would come to terms with their real situations and would protect their privilege by giving the tax-paying public the education it could be made to think it wanted for its children. Some steps in that direction were actually taken. The MLA, which less than ten years before had been insisting that composition must be taught in the schools, not the colleges, now began to urge English departments to protect their required freshman courses and thus their shrinking budgets; and some individual slick operators began to hedge their bets by *talking* about teaching composition, by teaching graduate students to teach what they still refused to teach themselves, or by building little empires of upper division composition classes limited to a dozen or so selected followers.

Most of the established didn't even go that far. Instead, the operators competed with one another in devising gimmicks which would make them look busy while in reality protecting their unique privilege. Advanced classes could always be multiplied or at least held at constant numbers by lowering the ceilings on enrollment, and TAs who had previously been forbidden to take more than two courses a semester could now be required to take three as a condition of continuing employment. It didn't matter if some of those courses rarely met and had no substantive content. As long as the students registered and paid their fees, funding formulas based on enrollments would keep the money rolling in.

One gallant invention in that gorgeous gallery was actually designed to get money from and for students who were taking no classes and weren't even on campus. It worked quite simply. Doctoral candidates were required to register and pay fees for every semester from admission-to-candidacy to attainment of their doctorates. In Texas, as you may know, for every hour of registration at the doctoral level in the liberal arts the Coordinating Board has recommended that in 1980 the Legislature assign a state university over $230 for its faculty's salaries. If a thousand or twelve hundred unregistered candidates could thus be required to register for three hours each for just one semester, the take for faculty salaries would be over $800,000. The Graduate Assembly at UT Austin has passed the continuous registration rule this very spring, and the notion that it involves a disgraceful conflict of interest has been received with undisguised hostility.

One other device for holding on to privilege while avoiding the indignity of teaching freshmen must still be mentioned, though I am sure that to many of you my whole sad recitation is old hat. Since Ph.D.s in English can't get jobs, intelligent students have become reluctant to enter our graduate programs, and without TAs the spectre of assignment to freshmen teaching becomes increasingly substantial. Hence the employment of what is called "the wage section" — faculty wives, unemployed Ph.D.s, graduate dropouts, and the like — who can be given short-term appointments with heavy loads at low wages but without hope of tenure. The big department of the future thus looms before us as sharply divided into the haves and the have-nots. Though the haves have spent years avoiding precisely the conditions they are now imposing on the have-nots, objections to sweated labor are also looked upon as trouble-making. The Profession seems bound and determined to expose its high moral pretenses as only that — pretenses. If ever again I hear a dean or a chairman talking about the wisdom of the race and the roots of our culture, I am going to throw up.

So there are the bones whose possible life is now at last to be considered. An aging Methodist must not irreverently question the power of the Lord to build the ruined places and to plant that which was desolate, but it would be foolish for the aged to expect that in their life-time *any* prophecy will set the bones to shaking and coming together with flesh upon them and breath in them. Realistically, the prospects for the humanities in the spiritually bankrupt state universities are dim; even the relatively wealthy

69

among private institutions are hurting for money — and some
are not overburdened with wisdom; and though I can't pretend
to know much about the junior colleges, they seem to have their
problems too. The son of a classicist and the grandson of
theologians, as an English professor I have to call myself a third-
generation loser.

In any estimate of our professional future, we have to begin
by writing off the comfortable struldbrugs. At least in the big
state universities, they won't teach freshmen or sophomores if
they can help it; and really neither old nor young among us know
much about teaching composition even if we want to. Learning
and teaching to write is nearly as mysterious as the acquisition of
language. A bibliography of the subject records great activity,
passionate conviction, but little proved accomplishment, so that
a specialist in composition may be defined as a specialist in
things hoped for, in the evidence of things not seen. So far as I
can tell after forty years of trying, most required comp-courses
don't justify the effort of giving them. The fad for rhetoric
(defined as anything so called) gives professors something to
pontificate about in abominable prose, the fad for "basic
writing" puts some chromium-strips on traditional grammar,
but I know that at UT Austin my own teaching of required
comp, whatever unseen changes it may work, produces just no
measurable results. For the past six or eight years, I have felt increasingly that a first step in the right direction would be to admit our limitations, to abolish required courses in English
altogether (as required courses in Greek and Latin were long
since abolished), and to offer as many of the most plausible elective courses in composition as we can manage and real demand
will justify. But that isn't going to happen. Academic inertia, the
foolish outcry about "the crisis in writing," and our own
knowledge that if requirements go the budget goes will keep the
freshman and sophomore courses limping along for the
foreseeable future.

Who will teach them? Some academic operators have
already sniffed out the coming racket, and the young have
already recognized that the sign "composition specialist" marks
the best avenue now open to employment in an English department. But administrators aren't going to forget the lesson we've

carefully taught them for the past twenty years — namely, that freshmen and sophomores can be taught as well by raw beginners as by veterans, and a lot more cheaply; and the now-threatened scientists will gobble up all the money that they can. As I have said, we have to expect that our departments will be populated by diminishing numbers of expensive literati and a growing crowd of miscellaneous wage-section people, a "resource pool" of hangers-on to academe, who for varied personal reasons will allow themselves to be exploited. More generally, in our advanced technological society there will be a tiny handful of big bosses, a somewhat larger group of pampered scientists and technologists (on campus and off), and a substantial number of moderately skilled underlings. English departments will be expected to make those underlings functionally literate. The rest of the population will go to one junkyard or another.

In this situation, the old and the middle-aged among us will scramble for themselves, since it is too late for them to change professions easily. The young should get out of English altogether unless they have what used to be talked of as a genuine calling. But there is nothing in all this to make old or young despair. The worst of all possible worlds is also the best, and since I don't have time to emphasize a shyly-wryly optimistic conclusion by moving toward it slowly, let me emphasize it by saltation.

There *are* young people who are called — middle-aged and aging people too. The pleasures of studying the English language and the literatures in it are as great as they ever were, though the material rewards are certainly declining; and it's possible to keep body and soul together by doing something else while continuing those studies. If one gets to teach, one can still help students learn to read and write if they really want to. We are really better off, right now, than we were before the disease of affluence infected us. Some of us, of all ages, do like to read and write and to help others learn to. Those pleasures, in whatever degree we are capable of them, are the things that matter to us as English teachers; and the organized cupidity which we call The Profession is at best a necessary evil and maybe not even necessary. If some strange visitation should suddenly wipe out all the machinery of deans and chairmen and committees and councils and lobbies and newsletters and conventions, if no more prizes were offered for Lilliputian leaping and creeping, still the things which I would like to be good enough to value would remain.

Ruth Zabriskie Temple was born December 26, 1908, in Passaic, New Jersey. Educated at Mount Holyoke, Radcliffe, Bryn Mawr, and Columbia, Professor Temple spent most of her teaching career at Brooklyn College. In 1973 she was named comparatist at the Graduate Center, City University of New York. She has served as a Fulbright professor of American literature at the University of Strasbourg. The title of her essay reflects the nature of some of her significant publications: "The Ivory Tower as Lighthouse in Edwardians and Late Victorians," and "Never Say I: *To the Lighthouse* as Vision and Confession."

Ruth Z. Temple

View From a Room in the Ivory Tower

I had first thought of my title as reading View from a Woman's Room in the Ivory Tower, but that raises all sorts of expectations I am not prepared to gratify. Besides, I want to suggest Virginia Woolf, not Marilyn French.

This academic year finds me half a century from my college graduation and, owing to my profession, some fifty-four years confined, if that is the word, in what used to be derisively called the ivory tower of Academe. Now, to be sure, my Academy has included fifteen institutions of higher learning, seven as student, eight as teacher (not all of these different), European and American universities, private women's colleges, and public (city) colleges. Besides that, like all academics, owing to the fringe benefits of professional congresses, lecture assignments, and the necessities of research, I have visited a multitude of campuses beyond my own. Scholars since Plato's day have been peripatetic; in the Middle Ages they wandered; now, constrictions of time impose jet travel. Perhaps the Ivory Tower does after all permit a world view.

My special theme will be the changes I have observed from my vantage point — changes in the Academy and the place of women in it. On the latter point I have a cautionary message to

75

Confronting Crisis

deliver. Many women today, bemused by their visibility, suffer the delusion that only NOW has their cause begun to prosper and therefore the only way is up. On the contrary — as I shall demonstrate. In the course of my tale I shall acknowledge some debts — the sort that never get discharged unless perhaps into some general fund there for humanity to draw on.

First beginnings are of course in the home. There it was taken for granted that I would "be" when I grew up whatever I wanted to. My physician father would have preferred the law for me (because he thought lawyers talked so well) and he warned only against obstetrics, as too physically demanding for women. When I went to college his sole stipulation was that I take Greek — so that I would learn to talk well. But before college and in some ways more important, there was my school, a small, uncelebrated private day school in my ordinary town, to which I went from first grade through high school, skipping two and a half years to save time. It was extraordinarily good, for the only reason that schools are good: it had a dedicated faculty assembled by a remarkable principal, Maud Brown. Principal and faculty were women, though the school was coeducational through grade nine. Miss Brown knew and acted on that elementary and neglected truth about the nature of developing minds: children learn easily and enjoy doing it. So we memorized the presidents of the United States, the kings of England, the outline of ancient and medieval history, and masses of poetry. Everything was expected of us: six hours daily of homework in high school, voluntary summer projects (I made a collection of pressed wild flowers and read all the French books in our local library). French was taught from the third grade, Latin for five years; from the fourth grade everyone was in the annual Shakespeare play. To that school I owe mastery of the one indispensable lesson: to learn is the most rewarding of all pursuits and the most essential. Before I left, I knew that I would be an English teacher — in high school, of course, like my role models there.

At Mount Holyoke College I had in my first year no teacher so good as they, but later on I had many excellent teachers, some of them distinguished scholars and all but three women (all but two department heads were women). I revised my career plan: I

76

would be a college teacher. There seemed to be no difficulty about that. Indeed, I might hope to be a college president, like Mary Woolley. Most of the Seven Sisters then had women presidents (this was 1925-29), a happy condition not always maintained but this year bettered: for once all seven are presided over by women. (The percentage of women college presidents in the United States today is seven.) Mary Woolley's contribution to Mount Holyoke has not even yet been fully assessed, nor has she had the biography she deserves. (The latest one, by Anna Mary Wells, is a disservice to her memory.) She made us all aware, there in a rural valley between the Galloping Hills, of the world of international diplomacy, of underprivileged regions, of jobs of work to be done by those so fortunate as to be well educated. In my senior year, my honors paper advisor taught me research and bibliographical method and how to make an index, skills for the teaching of which no provision was made in two of my three graduate schools. — Columbia was the exception and the teacher no less than the great reference librarian Isabel Mudge.

Equipped with a fellowship from Mount Holyoke for graduate study, I chose between Yale and Radcliffe on grounds of brevity: an M.A. could be got from Radcliffe in one year but Yale demanded two. At Radcliffe, shades of the prison house began to close about the growing female. I found that Harvard classes were not open to Radcliffe graduate students — except Gothic (I was one of two women in what seemed like thirty middle-aged men, boning up for their written doctorals in history of the language). I found that Widener stacks were not open to beginning Radcliffe graduate students except by permission of a professor for a special project. Radcliffe might indeed read at Widener — in a room known as the Black Hole of Calcutta. Even doctoral students, if they were women, were not allowed in Widener stacks after six o'clock. The legendary reason for this rule was that in the evening hours they might constitute temptation for the males, who were after all the University's principal concern. Never have I felt more surely a second class citizen than in the Harvard Yard. And I may say that very little has changed there. Of that more hereafter. (Later I was urged to join the Radcliffe Club of New York, with the privilege of using on special occasions a room at the Harvard Club — on

77

condition of entering the building through a special door. I declined.) I suppose I should add that my Harvard professors were up to their reputation. Lectures were admirable. And Widener — to which a professor did give me access — is my favorite library on both sides of the Atlantic.

Bryn Mawr, which I tried next, was totally different from Radcliffe. As there were only women students, undergraduate and graduate, there was no ground for discrimination. Of my four professors there only one was a man — and only one, Margaret Gilman, was of any use whatever. An authority on Baudelaire, she taught me a great deal about the use of evidence and how to write reports. She and only she of all the teachers I have had knew how to make a seminar profitable. In general, I deplore the seminar system as the exclusive teaching instrument in graduate schools. One does not learn much from the reports of one's peers — except patience. Of course in graduate school one is not taught; one learns. Reports, papers, examinations, even if not well criticized, as they often are not, are the instruments — the nights of anguished writing, the hours of talk. The library not the classroom is the heart of the matter. By accident of propinquity, my fellow scholars at Bryn Mawr provided what Radcliffe had not: a rewarding intellectual atmosphere. But Bryn Mawr rejected as too modern the dissertation subject I had long since determined on (the 1890s!), so I proceeded to Columbia. There I confirmed what I had suspected: graduate institutions, as contrasted with undergraduate, should be coeducational. And at Columbia one feels free. However, I must add that only one woman was lecturing in English (none in French) and she never made it to full professorship though she was an excellent scholar. The conspicuous advent of Marjorie Nicolson as full professor was later — and changed nothing except that fractional percentage point of female representation on the tenured staff. As my graduate study progressed, Columbia permitted me to direct master's theses (there was one other female in this category). But Columbia did continue my initiation into the hard reality of a discriminatory world. When I applied for admission, the department chairman welcomed me — on condition that I should not expect Columbia to get me a job. "I have," he said, "woman college presidents coming in and saying, 'I'll take a second-rate man

Ruth Z. Temple

in preference to a first-rate woman.' " This classic utterance, of the year 1933, needs, I think, to be recorded.

You will note that by now we are into the Great Depression. And, I think, from that dates the real decline in women's academic fortunes. The fact is indisputable; explanations vary. Even at Mount Holyoke, hitherto unusual for the high proportion of women on its staff, the situation changed. That was because the college had seen fit to celebrate its one hundredth birthday by appointing its first male president. (On her retirement, the principal of my school was also replaced by a mediocre man. The school has never recovered.) Holyoke's president at once set about bringing the ratio of male instructors up to the fifty per cent then current at Smith. Fifty percent! At this moment Holyoke has a very slight favorable edge over Smith which has full professors: 62 men to 22.33 women; associate professors: 45.50 men to 24.50 women; assistant professors: 39.50 men to 32.17 women; and in the lowest rank women as usual doing better, instructors: 13 men to 17.17 women. Smith has 15 male department heads to 12 female.

Of course in my time there were no openings for women at Harvard, Princeton, Yale. Here progress is being made, but barely. Women students are new to Yale and Princeton, and innovation more beneficial, perhaps, to the university than the women. Harvard is a special case, because Harvard always had Radcliffe students to be instructed — by men, separately until 1943, when Radcliffe students were let into some Harvard classes. The ratio of women freshman undergraduates to men at Harvard today is 1:1.8, owing to the new policy of Equal Access, but the chances that a Radcliffe woman might have one woman professor in her four years are minuscule. Affirmative Action has thus far produced (1978) 24 woman full professors out of 756 (compare this with 22 of 84 at Smith): 1 of 18 in English, 1 of 13 in Romance languages, in linguistics none at any rank, in physics one at the lowest rank. Lucky few. Or are they?

By and large, from the 1930s on, the academic path for women has been downhill all the way. In 1940 the percentage of women on all college faculties was 27; in 1970, 22; in 1977-79, 18.2 (full professors 5.8). The peak, towering high above 1939, was — in 1879. *Have* you come a long way, Baby? Further to

79

Confronting Crisis

frustrate complacency, note that in 1973-74 the percentage in France was 24, in the USSR, 52, though fewer of their women than of ours get Ph.D.s. So much for the argument, advanced in all official quarters, that women must wait for a more respectable faculty showing until they constitute a larger "labor pool." The percentage of Ph.D.s awarded to women is slowly going up but partly because men are getting fewer. It was 13.4 in 1970; 17.7 in 1975.

Looking at these figures I recognize how fortunate I have been in the accident of chronology — except in one respect. The academic crisis and recession of these years is for women unlike the Great Depression precisely because of Affirmative Action. If it is not paying very large dividends, at least it has created a climate of opinion in which discrimination has gone underground. *Feminist*, if controversial, is no longer a disreputable qualifier. In my early job-hunting years I was warned never to let it be suspected that I was that sinister thing. A male chairman, having observed my teaching of the three Greek Electra plays, remarked with a very nasty smile: "I seemed to detect feminism in your approach. Are you a feminist?" To students, even female students, feminism was just corny (though that word had not been invented): relic of a time when women maybe did have to struggle for rights long since secured — so forget it.

My apprenticeship to discrimination was proceeding. In my second tenure-line job, an elder stateswoman prophesied: You will be promoted, but only after all the men at your level have been. So it was. And so it had been with her — internationally known for years before the college found her a full professorship. Others of my female colleagues, fully qualified, retired as associates. This was at a New York City college, probably as coeducational colleges go among the least backward. Yet a few years ago a not unsophisticated or illiberal colleague at our graduate school asked me, phrasing his question for the answer he anticipated, "There is no discrimination against women at your college, is there?"

The presence and prosperity of woman on the academic scene has been an up and down thing and is likely to continue so, reflecting as the Academy itself does, public opinion and the state of the economy. Most things academic are cyclical. Old

80

birds like myself have had to learn, as a survival device, to tolerate the recurrent emergence through channels of a reformed curriculum masquerading as New but in fact long ago tried, evaluated, rejected. Curricula go from mandatory to permissive and back again. (Just now they are happily on their way back to basics after the capitulation to relevance occasioned by the historic student revolt.) The two-term freshman English requirement, standard for decades, gave way to one-term precisely as, through the disastrous inauguration of open admissions, the city colleges were flooded with the illiterate. As J.A. Spender said, "The longer I live the more I see that things really are as silly as they seem."

There is, however, one innovation — irreversible, I fear: the admission of women, some women, into the old established men's colleges and of men into some women's colleges — not, I am happy to say, any of the Six Sisters (Radcliffe in this context does not count) with the notorious exception of Vassar. It is highly unlikely that most women would profit by a Yale or an Amherst education (the degree is quite another thing) or most men by one at Vassar. Coeducational institutions we have never lacked in America and they serve their purpose very well. A woman's college with a handful of men or vice versa is neither fish nor flesh nor good red herring. The single-sex or segregated college has not only an honorable history but manifest advantages — at least for women. Statistically their graduates are twice as likely to succeed in careers as coeds; if both are married, three times; if the coed is married and the other not, seven times. In this last comparison lies concealed another lesson for women.

In brief, if you want to go up the academic ladder, take your cue from the Carnegie Report, *Opportunities for Women in Higher Education* (September 1973): do not let your graduate study be delayed or interrupted by child-bearing or child-rearing or anything else (such as, putting your husband through graduate school); do not lose geographical flexibility through marriage. One further statistical argument advanced by Elizabeth Tidball, the author of the study from which I have taken these ratios: the most significant factor in women's success is the ratio of women teachers to students. Maybe it was not such a bad idea for Mount Holyoke in its first hundred years to have had on its faculty far more women then men. And as in 1976 one-half of all women full professors in the United States were in women's colleges — though these make up only a small fraction of the total — if you want a teaching job, Sister, better boost women's colleges. That they work is no mystery. In those colleges women hold all the offices, win all the honors. For the first and last time they have been *primae inter pares* and the lords and masters of their fates and faces. If this is no microcosm of the great world, so much the better for those who have had one fling. Let us hope that diversity will continue to be seen as a good and that these "peculiar" institutions will long endure.

The phrase — *primae inter pares* — has been given renewed currency in the title of Elaine Kendall's unsatisfactory book on the Seven Sisters (1976). I am glad to find support for my view in the Carnegie report cited, a document generally deplorable for its bland and unconscious male chauvinism (two women to seventeen men on the Commission that produced it).

I said earlier that the Academy reflected the current state of society. If it only reflects and reflects only a lowest common denominator of popular thinking, then our civilization is doomed. There are uncomfortable signs of sinister deterioration in the American educational system. When I passed very demanding College Board entrance examinations, I could never by the exercise of all my imaginative powers have foreseen a day when with groans of apprehension an eighth-grade reading level test would be instituted as a requisite for a high school diploma and thus for college entrance. My own freshmen in the city colleges, in the forties and fifties, would most of them have made nothing of my father's fifth grade reader. But now my graduate students who have struggled to get a Ph.D. are, if they have any jobs at all, assigned to teach the functionally illiterate to write not, God help us, a research paper (standard freshman fare even in my undergraduate teaching days), not an essay, not even a paragraph, but a reasonably correct sentence. This jewel is one of the "paragraphs" from a 1978 freshman paper (the fourth written in the term) shown me by a former colleague: "University gaive one the uses of development field of study that one have, be it professal or mechainal." The paper was based on Newman's "Idea of a University," perhaps an unwise choice for the class in question. The last sentence-paragraph of the eight-sentence essay is revealing: "I do not get a whole understanding of the book I also did not finish reading the book."

The decline has reached the graduate schools. Students entering know much less than would formerly have been judged adequate and they resist the acquisition of facts. Let one date appear in a doctoral examination question and a howl of indignation arises. The under-furnished mind like the under-furnished house is modish: more is less. Yet scholarship is before anything a fact-finding enterprise (*der liebe Gott steckt im Detail*). The craft, passed on in the West by medieval clerics who saved for us the records of the past (without past no civilization), is in danger of withering away. I speak of the humanities. Apprentices to science still activate Carlyle's prediction: There shall be much running to and fro and knowledge shall be increased. But knowledge of the past is the business of humanities, and if, following strange gods, they neglect the fruitful study of history and literature and the history of literature, we shall suffer the fate foretold by Santayana: Those who ignore the past are condemned to repeat its errors.

As our century declines, we discern in our decadence alarming parallels to the decadence of imperial Rome. In case what follows seems disproportionate in space or strident in tone, I must plead the compulsion of age. "Old people," says Eudora Welty's homely philosopher in *Losing Battles*, "want to tell us what's on their mind, regardless of what it is or who wants very bad to know it."

Our public institutions are in disarray: the established churches, constitutional democracy, the family. Young adults sue their parents for malpractice while psychiatrists assure middle-aged children that they need feel no guilt for abandoning their parents to the care of volunteers and the state. For ethics is substituted behavioral modification. Commercial dogfights are ten times more prevalent than ten years ago; agribusiness with its inhumanity to animals proliferates; thirty million people in this "scientific" age believe in astrology; some twenty-five million subscribe to cults, whose only validation is a founder, usually shady. The progressive debasement of language is everywhere observable, even in the Academy, and in no respect more exasperating than in the epidemic verbal tic: *you know*. Odd, because we never do. Narcissism is in fashion: Who am I? is the vapid and unanswerable question that preoccupies disoriented adolescents and adults. Man the great predator is finishing off at an alarming rate his fellow-inhabitants of the globe. Man the exploiter proceeds day by day to render his planet uninhabitable, now and forever, stock-piling nuclear bombs, accumulating nuclear and toxic wastes, corrupting earth, air, and water, and impairing the ozone. Meanwhile, with characteristic inconsequence, he prepares the "conquest" of space.

Most of these enterprises have been brought within our grasp by technology — here we have improved upon the Romans and by so much our decadence exceeds theirs. But we owe technology to science and science ultimately depends on reason, the *faculté maîtresse* that from Plato onwards has been seen as man's peculiar distinction. Yet it is an abandonment of reason that marks our present decadence just as it marked that of Rome. In the nourishment of reason, what exemplary role is the Academy now playing? What indeed.

For a teacher of literature, the flight from reason is deplorably manifest in the arts and the art of criticism. Modernism is dwindling, it appears, into Post-Modernism. So one hears at conferences devoted to the vain pursuit of a label more precise for the vacancy about us. The retrospective view, it appears, is now appropriate. And how enchanting is that view.

To have shared the world with great artists, to have "taught" them while their work was taking shape (how Eliot deplored being pinned wriggling into the curriculum while still alive), is a happy accident, and I rejoice that mine were not, say, George Eliot and Carlyle, but T. S. Eliot, Auden, Virginia Woolf. The first two were part of my New York academic scene. Perhaps my single most memorable experience in the theatre was *The Cocktail Party* on Broadway, not the first night, attended, I suppose, by the press and the beautiful people, but the second, to which had come the entire academic community of greater New York. Never have I felt so keen a rapport between stage and house. (Of the same order was the second night of Beckett's *Waiting for Godot* with Bert Lahr.) We heard from year to year "Prufrock," "The Waste Land," "Marina," in the poet's voice, at the 92nd St. YMCA — his favorite audience, he used to tell us. By then J. Alfred Prufrock's creator had grown into Old Possum, elderly, quizzical, not un-American uncle, who refrained from comment on his texts because, he said, everyone else knew much more than he about them. Auden I heard first just off the boat, arrived to change fatherlands. At a dinner to raise money for the Spanish Loyalists, this subject of His Britannic Majesty exhorted us in his Oxford accent to forsake the class-structured society for the democratic — not, some of his audience felt, a topic on which he could well instruct America. But he became our neighbor. I even lived in a Brooklyn Heights apartment that he had earlier occupied, leaving as tokens of his residence cigarette burns in the parquet floor. His poetry, too, we savored in the poet's voice, along with Frost's and William Carlos Williams'. There is now no major poet in England or America.

Nor is there to be had the excitement I used to feel on the appearance of the annual volume of Jules Romains' *Hommes de bonne volonté* and the less frequent novels of Ivy Compton-Burnett. (I cannot, I fear, take a comparable pleasure in Iris Murdoch's yearly variation on a melodramatic dance to the music of sex.)

My ambulatory ivory tower having been stationed for the longest time in or near the city, the New York stage was my privileged view. Infinite riches in rather too much room (one spent endless transit hours underground): the Lunt-Fontanne gamut, Eva Le Gallienne's two repertory theaters, Jane Cowl as Juliet, Ruth Gordon as the country wife, Cornelia Otis Skinner in *The Way of the World*, Nazimova in *The Cherry Orchard*, and, season after season, Martin Green, irreplaceable star of the D'Oyly Carte Company, with his physical and verbal acrobatics. Even more special were Gertrude Stein's and Virgil Thomson's *Four Saints in Three Acts* and, at the grand old Metropolitan Opera House, Cocteau's and Stravinsky's version of *Oedipus Rex*. One season there were three competing Hamlets — Gielgud's my preference.

Current events were cataclysmic, but never have there been such funny comedies: *Life with Father*, *You Can't Take It With You*, *Arsenic and Old Lace*, and, funniest of all, *The Male Animal* with and by Elliot Nugent and the one and only, the incomparable James Thurber, New Yorker cartoonist, fabulist, writer of American prose equalled only by that of E. B. White. (An infallible antidote to a dim view of Modernism is Thurber's *My Life and Hard Times*.) Now we import our comedies from England and very funny they are but the humor is grey if not black. Also, they demand English actors and English precision of utterance. Drama, especially comic, in France and England, is the art form in healthiest shape today, along with the innovative French novel. But Modernism in America gave us the musical comedy, as distinctive in the twentieth century as American railroad stations in the nineteenth. The gems which my generation saw first are still current fare (though some of the landmark stations have disappeared): from *Pins and Needles* and *Pal Joey* through *Oklahoma*, along with Shaw's unwitting contribution, *My Fair Lady*, and Noel Coward's cornucopia. On the screen were Greta Garbo, incomparable actress, and Marlene Dietrich, incomparable seductress. Noah Greenberg's Pro Musica was recreating medieval and Renaissance music, with Russell Oberlin, and at the galleries were Georgia O'Keefe, Edward Hopper, John Marin, all artists in progress. These were Modernism, and of those days one can indeed say, Bliss was it then to be alive,/And to be young was very heaven.

On the bleak current scene, sole redemption of Post-Modernism, is Samuel Beckett, superlative artist in two languages and three or four media. Beckett is the artist for our present time, his anti-heroes the heroic embodiment of the human condition in this whimpering world: "I can't go on I'll go on." Who and what else is there? Commercial TV to provide amusement for the culturally disabled, art in which interest has replaced beauty. Electronic music substitutes noise for harmony; a visual object may be an earthwork deforming the desert or an assemblage of scrap metal and dirty rags, a poem an incoherent assemblage of banal words conveying, if anything, narcissistic confession.

To deal with the literature of Post-Modernism, what instrument does the Academy furnish us? One that repudiates history and denies literature in the traditional sense, and in this denial and repudiation serves the cause not of civilization but of barbarism, of anti-reason. The new critical mode, structuralism or post-structuralism (I discern no difference) excites variously awe, amusement or dismay. From me, after a lifetime of devotion to "the gay science," it wrings the ancient Irish lament: The periwinkle and the tough dogfish / At eventide have got into my dish.

Modernism invented New Criticism, a largely American creation though I. A. Richards was a founding father. To the literature of our time it was a useful handmaid, for it encouraged explication of the difficult but not opaque texts. I rejoice in the accident of chronology that made it for me the routine teaching device.

Structuralist criticism, which has displaced it, is an importation from France. Adopting or adapting first principles from linguistics and anthropology, with some admixture of Freud, the French play about in the empyrean of speculation, sporting with the shade of Descartes. The Americans lumber after, inventing nothing. They have already trailed the French through existentialism and phenomenology; now they follow the gospel according to Lacan, Foucault, Derrida. And, aping science, they invent a jargon, a metalanguage, which makes their pronouncements rebarbative if not impenetrable. (Science, of course, has its own eloquence: precision, clarity, rational development. Do not expect these from structuralism.) Roland Barthes, repenting one of his phases, puts it nicely: *"J'ai cru alors avec ardeur à la possibilité de m'intégrer à une science sémiologique. J'ai traversé un rêve (euphorique) de scientificité."* Our American structuralists have not awakened from their euphoric dream of scientificity. One must, they say, read in a "writerly" not a "readerly" way. That is, one should not attempt to discover what Dante or Baudelaire said, but "strongly misread" these masters. We must, in fact, "deconstruct" or "benignly violate" their texts. Explicate at your peril. "If interpretation can never accomplish itself, it is simply because there is nothing to interpret." Thus Foucault. And he goes on: "Interpretation will always henceforth be an interpretation by the 'who'. One does not interpret that which is a signified but in the last analysis the one 'who' has laid down the interpretation. The principle of interpretation is nothing but the interpreter himself." Instead of explication, then, we have exercises in sheer or mere ingenuity. In "An Enormity for Flaubert:

Confronting Crisis

Exercises in Semiotic Foreplay," Robert Chumbley constructs an "abduction" about *Trois Contes* and proceeds through eleven meaningless pages to conclude with diagrams of three cones which he has discerned as deep structures of the tales. It is not, of course, claimed that these were any part of Flaubert's intention or that they could have been discerned by any reader other than Chumbley, or that, having been discerned, they contribute in any way to our enjoyment or understanding of *Trois Contes*. The exercises led to nothing. (Was "foreplay" the *mot juste*?) The corruption is spreading. A recent analyst of college entrance examinations deplores the persistent reflection of New Criticism in the tests, outmoded method dating back to the 1930s and 1940s, and calls for an update to include "the structuralism coming out of New Haven." Here are some of the delicacies the student of literature is now offered by the Indiana Press. One book will tell us about "the crucial roles of intertextuality and of the overdetermination of poetic discourse." Another "views literature from a semiotic standpoint, that is, as an information system employed for communication ends" and deals with "the manner in which the sender may be coupled with the receiver . . . the construct of the hypersign and genres as a coding program." Thus the vocabulary of a pseudo-technology debases the pursuit of literature. One longs for a Pope to enshrine these pedants in a new *Dunciad* or a Voltaire to impale them on this *pointe assassine*. That this like other vanities will pass is little comfort, for while it lasts it upholds the rule of anti-reason, the realm of chaos and old night. Moreover, as at least two graduate schools have become enclaves of this solemn foolery, its perpetuation for some little time is ensured. Even when the French have repudiated their creation and devised new literary games, young American instructors who have as graduate students picked up the ritual and dogma of structuralism will be passing them on to hapless freshmen as received truth. Thus the Academy aids and abets decadence as it connives in the non-teaching of our literary heritage. In the Academy as in the polis, the sleep of reason breedeth monsters. Populated by these, the landscape in my view now takes on the qualities of nightmare. This, in the century's decline, is, as Beckett shows us, How It Is.

Lewis Leary was born April 18, 1906, in Blauvelt, New York. His highest degree was bestowed by Columbia, and his teaching career has taken him to Beirut and back to Miami, Duke, Columbia, and finally the University of North Carolina, Chapel Hill. He was an officer in Strategic Service from 1942 to 1945 and served as English consultant for the United States Office of Education in 1965 and 1966. His numerous publications on American literary figures range from colonial writers to William Faulkner, and his compilation of articles on American literature between 1900 and 1968 is indispensable to scholars.

Lewis Leary

Grumble, Grumble, Toil or Tumble

I have been a student of literature for more than fifty years and have enjoyed every day of it. During the course of those years I have met many people of diverse kinds, other teachers and several generations of students. With a few prominent exceptions, my favorites have been among the latter. Some of them became teachers also, even deans and provosts, and at least one a university president. Others, and among the better, became professional football players or joined the tennis circuit. Still others became writers, journalists, poets (one of them an all-conference offensive lineman), and novelists, including a winner of the Pulitzer prize for fiction. Others of course are business or professional people, several of the more successful of whom have become book collectors — these I count among those with whom I have best succeeded. For it has been my opinion that the test of any teaching is not how well students do among the pressures of the classroom, but what they carry away from it and how long what they carry away lasts. Perhaps examinations should be postponed until, let's say, five years after a course is over. Then it may be discovered that that C- student who dozed on the back row and who accumulated more cuts than regulations allow, proves somehow to have gained more than any of the rest.

Confronting Crisis

That opinion, like almost any other, is based on personal experience. I have always had great sympathy for those who do not come to classes, wondering whether the fault has not been mine. Let me attempt to explain why. I did not do badly in college, though I was what now would be called a jock, working my impoverished way on an athletic scholarship. At the beginning of my sophomore year I decided that some classes were not worth the time spent in them, so instituted a one-man program of academic reform, with the result that before the term was two months old I had accumulated an enviable total of eighty absences. This not pleasing the dean, I was instantly placed on probation. Happily an amiable psychiatrist testified to my sanity and somewhat dubious good intentions, so that the ban was removed just in time for me to take my accustomed place at right end in the next Saturday's game. I learned something from that.

What else I learned in college, I am hard put at this time to recall. I do remember that ontogeny recapitulates phylogeny, that and nothing more. But I did learn attitudes, particularly from four dedicated teachers. One was a biologist, another a philosopher, the third a teacher of writing who sardonically slashed strings of adjectives from what I wrote and who warned against using words ending in *ion* because they deadened prose; only the fourth was a teacher of literature, and I did not really discover him until my senior year.

From the first I learned the primary secret of scholarship, that one must be immersed completely in what one is doing — he crossbred violets for, I suspect, some thirty years. From the second I learned humility, for I was fascinated by but understood hardly a word of what he said. The third taught discipline, a virtue, if it is a virtue, in the pursuit of which I have often been the least virtuous. From the fourth, I learned enthusiasm. These four — concentration, humility, discipline, and enthusiasm — have since seemed to me a pretty solid four-square foundation on which to build an education.

For education is not training. An animal may be trained. A machine can accumulate facts. Education is a leading out. When I grumble about my profession, the grumbling is about the emphasis we put on fact, what Emerson called the shining angularity of fact. Facts, of course, are stepping stones toward

Lewis Leary

knowledge. We would be hard put without them, but they are not, as some of my teachers and some of my associates have seemed to suppose them, the be all and end all of scholarship. But back now to my voyaging toward what I prefer to call critical scholarship, and what teaching can do to or for it. On graduation, I was offered two positions, one in biology (my major), the other in literature. The first would keep me at home; the second offered opportunity to teach abroad. Two roads diverging, I chose the one I could travel by. Three years went gayly past. Almost everything that I learned was intangible — I say almost everything because I spent much of the evening before my first class would meet cramming up on the difference between an adjective and an adverb, a distinction that I have since forgotten, except that I usually use them correctly, and even did before I spent those hours learning the difference between them. That, I think, also taught me something.

Reading is what I did then, discovering James Joyce, Virginia Woolf, Ezra Pound, William Faulkner, and Henry James, people who in my undergraduate days were seldom talked about. I read them avidly, joyously, with no concern about where they came from nor with any interest in prying into their private lives. That habit and conviviality, two virtues that I have been unwilling to forego, have sustained me ever since. And with them, the joy of teaching. If you don't love 'em, you can't learn 'em, advised my professor of English when I told him that I would teach, at the same time that he warned that if I were to continue in such occupation, I must either have an independent income or marry a wealthy wife. His advice I have not found difficult to follow, but his warnings, the first by circumstance, the second by superior choice, were disregarded. I would be a poet, and have been ever since, though seldom emerging from a closet. I would live in attic, with wine and a crust, and a patient companion beside me.

Instead, I was to find myself in a basement, with short share of wine or its equivalent, with little butter for my bread, but with a companion beyond compare. I had returned from abroad in the midst of the depression of the early 1930s. I had stumbled from one publishing house, one literary weekly, even one newspaper after another, offering my talent. I read poetry over

93

the radio to improve my image. I sent verse to small magazines to guarantee my reputation. But fame seemed certainly not ready to receive me. All else failing, I became manager of an apartment building, a converted brownstone residence not far from a university. The manager lived rent free in what had been the basement kitchen and servants' quarters. He stoked the furnace, he repainted, reupholstered, repaired plumbing, and did what he could to keep the house filled. For this he received fifty dollars a month. With time, he thought, on his hands, he enrolled, promising to pay later, in courses at the university. He attended few of them.

But finally fortune had come to the landlord. Three girls moved into the third-floor back apartment, and five weeks later, after what seemed then a necessary visit to City Hall for a certificate of marriage, one of them joined him in the basement apartment. Life has not been the same since. She began then, and has continued for now some forty-seven years, a campaign of encouragement and assistance and reform. Odd jobs were found, the most lucrative at forty cents an hour. The bill for tuition was paid. Willy-nilly, going to classes or not, the landlord became a fledgling graduate student.

But graduate study in the early 1930s seemed to him in most respects to have been a disaster. In no course that he took was literature talked about. One learned dates, necessary things of course, and one sat through lectures about writers, what they wrote and when they wrote and who had influenced whom. Professors were secluded beyond student reach behind closed doors. One, of superb honesty, read at first meeting of his course the list of books from which his lectures would be drawn, and suggested that students would be better advised to spend their time in the library reading those books than in listening to him condense and codify them. When it was discovered that another's lectures were drawn verbatim from the *Dictionary of National Biography*, there seemed, though he did not say so, little reason for attending his classes either. Philology? The first half of *Beowulf* was read word by parsed word. Few in the class read farther, to see how the story ended. One thing was certainly learned: never, said the landlord, would he teach like that.

And with some reasonable exceptions, he has remained true

to that vow. During his graduate school years he fell under the spell of one professor, so urbane, so polished, so close to the beau ideal of what a professor might be, that the landlord sat in on his course in medieval culture during each of the three years of his residence as a student, filling boxes full of note cards that were to stand him in good stead. For in the mid 1930s, wonder of all wonders, having slid through his preliminary doctoral examinations, he was offered a position, and anyone who remembers those parlous depression times knows that positions (jobs, we called them, and rightly so) for putative Ph.D.s were as difficult to come on as they are now.

The position found was in a very small department. It was made up of himself, the Professor, and the Dean of Women who taught half time. Shakespeare, Romantic literature, and American literature were under sole command of the Professor. The Dean of Women taught a sophomore survey. Everything else fell within the province of the landlord become instructor. He fed for almost five years from those boxes of note cards on medieval culture, in courses in Chaucer, medieval literature, the history of the English language, and Anglo-Saxon — the last a joy to teach, for in few other courses in any curriculum is the student's mind more a tabula rasa. Beyond that, he was in charge of as many sections, sometimes of sixty students, as were necessary in freshman composition. To fill his day, there was a course in journalism, another in epic poetry — the latter again sustained by those boxes full of notes.

Nine courses made up his normal load, twenty-seven classroom hours each week, and he took home joyfully a little over one hundred dollars a month, gladly teaching. Tenure? No one knew from one year to the next whether the University itself would survive. (It did, swollen now to gigantic proportions.)

Threatened with a deanship — after all, most of his afternoons were free — and with a Ph.D. now firmly in hand, he moved then to a larger institution at a salary just a little over three times that which he had first received. And there he learned about something called tenure, which he did not have. War came, and he was sent abroad on government service and his salary escalated to something more than the three times more than the three times more he had first received. The war over, he returned to teaching at exactly what he had been paid before he had left almost five years earlier. But he was happy, for he had learned that he did not have to teach, that there were other more remunerative occupations available. Whatever else, he was not stuck in a quagmire. Or was he?

For held over his head then was the bugaboo called tenure. He finally did receive it, in a quite adventitious manner that need not be gone into here, for though it was in another institution than those in which he later gladly served, the wretch who managed it is not dead. Suffice it to say that it brought him little popularity among colleagues of his own age. But he was of the elect; he was in and he could not be ousted. In the shade of the protective umbrella called tenure he discovered guaranteed security. An end or a new beginning?

With Thoreau, now allow me to confess that "I should not talk so much about myself if there were anyone else I knew as well." And with him I would address my remarks to poor students, to those among us now who do lead lives of quiet desperation. I would join them in their grumbling, for I have grumbled long and perhaps fecklessly as I have rebelled against my generation. If my rebellion has sometimes been less rigorous than it could have been, if I have succumbed to self-serving adherence to the adage, If you can't beat them, join them, then to whatever degree such accusations are correct, I have erred. But I would counsel patience also and suggest that nothing will release them from the quagmire in which many now seem fast stuck but willingness to accept whatever place can be found for them and through unceasing, honest toil to help rid their profession of its all too contagious ills.

As a not completely unscarred veteran of academic warfare, I have long been unashamedly a grumbler. I grumble about tenure as a debilitating temptation to mediocrity, wondering whether periodically, perhaps every ten years, let's say in each year ending in a zero, every department should have opportunity to have what Thoreau called a busk — a housecleaning in which useless or simply decorative objects can be discarded. I grumble also that students are too often talked to and not talked with. I grumble about the time-wasting ritual of taking attendance. I grumble especially that graduate study of literature has remained more drudgery than adventure, that graduate students are so often tested that they have little opportunity to learn, so that guides to literature become necessarily more important than literature itself. I grumble very loudly about what is done to teaching assistants, that corps of slave laborers who relieve professors from tasks considered onerous. I holler in indignation that more students are admitted to and allowed to complete graduate study than the job market can assimilate.

I have grumbled publicly about the temptations held forth to untenured people among us to rush toward shelter in response to the ancient rubric that publication prevents perishing. So much stuff is being printed in our proliferating semi-pro publications that bibliographies become the size of unabridged dictionaries. And much of it is unnecessary, repetitious, nit-picking. Though more is being published now than ever before that is discriminating and sound, it is so buried beneath the avalanche of petty, understandably self-serving small things that talking about literature often seems more babble than beneficial. I have elsewhere suggested that though picking at nits may be a healthful, even a pleasant occupation, it need not be done in public. Heads up!

But turn the coin. I grumble also that busyness has become a touchstone. What committees are served on, what academic chores are undertaken (and for whom), what educational innovations are worked out in long hours of conference — these good perhaps, certainly necessary things, have become pathways to security. Unions may be formed, strikes suggested, the paternal shade of protective associations sought. Disliking clerical work, one may become what is called a good teacher. My grumbling about that is less from jealousy than fear. What is more dangerous than the attractive teacher, sometimes master of what has been called the higher vaudeville, who has had so little time or inclination to keep up with his subject that he charmingly provides misinformation? Beware the brilliant teacher!

In this pitching of pennies, my heart does indeed rebel against my generation that has condoned and encouraged it. In vain the grumbling that the Ph.D. provides only an impressive hood to give color to academic processions. But grumbling briefly stops when I recall with pride that one university in which I have recently served has had enough self-confidence to appoint to a professorship a person with no academic degree at all and that in another there were five professors with no degree higher than that of a master of arts, and each a dedicated scholar, teacher, and critic. Each taught underclassmen and upper classmen, and most of them graduate students also. Nor were their hands dirtied as they performed necessary extracurricular chores.

But beyond that, each, of whichever sex, was a workman, committed to literature. All made their way without dissembling, in honesty, with patience. And my best fond hope for those who follow me in the profession that, for all my grumbling, has sustained me for many years is that, decorated with a doctorate or not, they seek out their own ways.

These again are parlous times. Discouragement and disappointment have deprived us of some of our more promising people who, with doctorate in hand, have sought surer security in law school or medical school or in business, becoming perhaps better lawyers or doctors or business persons because of years, which may seem wasted perhaps, among the humanities. Some will return, some will not and I grumble about that also. For never, I think, have the humanities needed greater intelligent support than now.

They are hedged about with hardships, many of their own making. They ride side-saddle through an obstacle course rutted with tradition and soggy with neglect. Ends are clouded. Means are confused. A once bright landscape is dimmed to myopic eyes. Other equestrians, better mounted, pass them at brisk gallop, more attractively accoutered, to capture trophies for a race well run. In vain the grumbling that times are out of joint. To gain audience, the arts don cap and bells or coyly strip-tease to prove their humanity. The anti-hero and the anti-humanist hold center stage. The best that is thought and said is incubated in other minds and finds expression in other voices. But a conviction remains that, grumble as we will, the humanities are not dead. Their sleep, if it is sleep, is not however one from which some charming prince can awaken them.

Sleeves rolled, they may yet rediscover trails from past to present, for every student of the humanities must speak to his or her time in terms understood. No mumbling, nor feckless grumbling either. Wondrous mausoleums of former achievement no longer attract contemporary attention. The house of intellect inherited from the past waits to be repaired, new additions added, the roof raised, the cellar deepened, the doorways widened. The servant of the humanities must throw aside shrouds of vocabulary within which arcane restatements lie lifeless, admired only by those who scatter incense to conceal evidence that, alas, the words are dead. He and she must speak up, speak out, and speak plainly to break bonds with which tradition has shackled scholarship. They will not join hands to sing sad grumbling songs, but will add a corrective voice that may, just may, bring to harmony the attractive single melodies provided by other disciplines.

My grumbling will not do it, nor yours either. My confidence remains, however, that it will be done, perhaps not by you nor me, but by someone, or perhaps by many, whom we have had the opportunity of leading out to recognition that there is greatly more to intellectual endeavor than getting degrees by sitting passive in a classroom or enjoying the shade of professional security.

Dorothy Bethurum Loomis calls herself an educator. Born in Franklin, Tennessee, April 5, 1897, she is a graduate of Vanderbilt with advanced degrees from Yale and Lawrence College. She is Phi Beta Kappa, has been a Fulbright fellow at Oxford, a fellow of the Guggenheim Foundation and the American Council of Learned Societies. To her extensive research in medieval, English, and American literatures, she now adds "some ideas I have about teaching English and about higher education in general."

Dorothy B. Loomis

No Better Gift of Fortune

It is impossible to lay down rules or write a prescription for producing a good teacher, for every teacher's success is unique, a product of his or her own learning and talents. But I think it safe to say that two things are essential to all good teaching: a love of learning and a strong desire to awaken that love in students, to communicate the values the teacher sees in literature or art or history or whatever is being dealt with. He or she must know how to study and continually enlarge the range of knowledge and perception, and must be sufficiently aware of the students to make them want to learn. Methods of achieving this end may differ. Some teachers perform best in formal lectures without any discussion from a class, while some do best with a Socratic give and take between teacher and student, and some with a combination of both. In any case the instructor should now and then give his students an example of a well organized and well delivered explication. Even discussions, though they may follow unexpected leads, ought to be recognizably organized around central points. I will try to describe my own method, faulty as it may at times have been.

When I was very young and just beginning to teach, I prepared a formal lecture for nearly every class and gave it without asking for student reaction. Perhaps I was afraid! Little by little I abandoned that practice, for I realized more and more that I needed to know what students were thinking, and they needed a forum for discussion. Suppose, for example, a student completely disagrees with your view of Gertrude's behavior in *Hamlet*. Must he sit there and swallow it without a chance to say to you and to his fellows how wrong he thinks you are? Surely not. In my experience the whole class profits by open discussion of such questions, and they may lead, as in this case, to useful investigations, for the student who finds Gertrude inconsistent can read the two quartos of *Hamlet* and compare Gertrude's role with that in the Folio to see how it developed. The danger in such a method is that if the teacher tries to involve most of the class in discussion, he will be likely to prod some students who find public expression painful or inappropriate. I remember teaching Shakespeare to a rather large class in a summer session at Harvard. About half the class were regular Harvard students, whom I found reluctant to talk. Finally my assistant, a graduate student, told me, "If you ask a Harvard man what he thinks, he regards it as an invasion of his privacy." Most students do not take that view, however, and on the whole I have found it the most successful way to bring literature to life in the classroom.

The responsibility of a teacher is twofold. He must pass on to a coming generation the learning of which he is supposedly a master, and he must add to the store of knowledge, either by the discovery of new facts or by new interpretations. Obviously I am talking about teaching and research. These two activities do not compete with each other; they reinforce each other, and the popular fallacy that they do not, that a teacher must choose between them, is based on ignorance. In a long life spent in the profession I have known only two good scholars who could not teach, and they could not, not because they spent their time in research, but because they were insensitive to their students, in one case not perceiving the fog of apathy in the classroom, in the other not knowing how to study to prepare for a class. I have never known a good teacher who was not a learned one.

It almost goes without saying that to keep alive a teacher must be working at his own level as well as at that of his students. Otherwise his powers decline and his stock of ideas runs low. And students like to think that their professors are well occupied, working as hard or harder at their own writing as the student is on his term paper. I could never effectively criticize a student's paper if I did not know from painful experience how difficult writing is. It is the hardest work I know anything about. Not all good teachers write, but most do. Those who do not undergo a similar discipline as they organize their knowledge, and it usually takes the spur of having to put words on paper to make them do this.

The joy of discovery! I know of nothing like it, nothing so explosively stimulating as finding out something for the first time — a significant new fact, the meaning of a document that has been misunderstood, or the meaning of a literary passage or historical fact. I can remember one small incident that gave me much pleasure. There was a document in late Old English that I had studied rather casually for many years, feeling that it contained something important, though I had never worked on it directly. Finally when I had to produce an article on something in that period, I decided to attack this document head on. I worked for quite a while before I saw its significance. When I finally did and wrote the last sentence of the article, I was so exhilarated that, though it was January and snow lay deep on the ground, I put on my boots and took a long walk in the woods, kept warm by the excitement of the discovery. The article I had written was not remotely connected with Chaucer, but I am sure I taught my Chaucer class better the next day for having worked through this problem. Similarly stimulating and valuable for teaching is a deepened knowledge of the meaning of a passage in a play or poem, the kind of awareness that sometimes comes suddenly but is usually the result of long study of the work. I remember being almost as excited when I thought I first saw what made Leontes turn against Hermione and Polixenes in the *Winter's Tale.*

I have said that the teacher must be equipped first with the love of truth and a passion for seeking it, and that is what research is all about. He studies because he wants to know. What he should somehow impart to his students is that a disinterested search for facts and truth is not without passion and is indeed the most valuable equipment anyone can have for living a decent

103

life. By one means or another we must encourage in our students — as well as in ourselves — an ever-increasing role of the intellect in one's life. This is no easy task, for we are a welter of churning emotions that lead, not to a calm assessment of evidence, but to impulsive opinion and action, whence comes the disheartening spectacle of supposedly educated people acting with the violence of prejudice and a scornful indifference to evidence. Perhaps the best cure is lifting both thought and emotion to as high a plane as possible, and here the humanities are our help.

The mind needs to be stored with thought, with ideas about the universe, both large and small, and of course the principal source of ideas is books. What the teacher should never forget is that it is in school, college, and university that one learns to refuse to settle for second-rate "easy" reading, for books whose ideas are so pale they wash out in any real encounter with life. For various reasons I would not make a curriculum of Great Books nor insist that all students study philosophy, but I would insist that the teacher's responsibility is to try to create in his students an appetite that cannot be satisfied by the daily paper, the weekly magazine, or the TV screen. Anyone who has worked through Plato's Socratic dialogues, Dante's *Divine Comedy*, Montaigne's *Essays*, Shakespeare's plays has enjoyed a fare that should create a reliable desire for continued refreshment. Such fare should not be diluted with trivia.

And here I would make another plea. I think it is the duty of teachers of literature to familiarize themselves with all the great works of western letters, as far as possible in the language in which they were written. It is worth learning Greek to be able to read Homer. But in a profession of multitudinous demands I must admit one cannot bring all western languages to a degree of competence that will enable one to read with appreciation all the great works. Somewhere we must settle for translations, but we should always be aware that it is a second-best choice. To show the difference between an original and a translation, we can have a student read *Hamlet* in French or *Midsummer-Night's Dream* in German. Furthermore, to counter the present disgraceful neglect of foreign languages, we must show our students that they are pitifully limited in the knowledge of how other minds

Dorothy B. Loomis

work, painfully provincial in outlook, as long as they have no proficiency in foreign languages. As far as English literature is concerned, to take only a very obvious example, a person ignorant of Vergil can never know Milton.

I have been writing as if a teacher's sole responsibility was to his classroom and to his research. There is another dimension to his job, and that is to do his share of keeping the works of the machinery of the university in good condition and not leave it all to the administration. The supposed nostalgic desire of "real teachers" is simplicity, Mark Hopkins on one end of the log and the student on the other. But, alas, the good old days are gone, and the recent explosion of the demands society makes on a university render such simplicity no longer possible. In the interest of protecting education itself from the clamoring voices from outside its walls asking help with social services, slum planning, community concerts, and adult education, there must be a body of people whose duty it is to deal with these demands, by deflecting or satisfying them. Hence the proliferation of deans, vice-presidents, and provosts. I think as much as possible of this business should be left to them. But there is the curriculum, student grants, the college calendar, and, alas, other matters on which the faculty must speak, and I now mean those time-consuming committees. A conscientious teacher has to take his share of these duties. But here a real danger emerges. Acting on important committees gives the participant a sense of power and of satisfaction, which is innocent enough in itself. But it is all too easy to let the proliferation of committee duties take the place of study and research. Onerous as they often are, committee duties are easier than writing a few pages of an article, and unhappily professors sometimes grow to prefer them. Periodically in almost any college or university there is a cry to do away with some of the committees, but when it comes down to the scratch each one will have its supporters who find it absolutely necessary to the health of the institution, and there will be found willing souls to man it. Any individual teacher must learn to balance all these duties and to realize that, valuable as his wisdom may be on these many matters, it is not absolutely essential to the survival of the institution.

In spite of the formidable organization of learning, it is still

105

simplicity that we need. It is in the classroom that the stifling effect of this complex organization must be overcome and the student brought face to face with learning. Let the registrar struggle with records and computers, the deans with allocation of funds, the teacher and the student are at the heart of the process, an examination of man's finest achievements. No matter how much red tape is necessary before the student reaches the classroom, here it must be completely obliterated, and that is the salvation of the university's wheels within wheels, the end for which they turn. Sometimes I think college presidents, under the pressure of keeping the institution solvent, forget that fact and think the projection of a good image before the community is the important thing.

The teacher of the humanities, whether it be literature, art, history, philosophy, or perhaps science is carrying a particular responsibility today, and that is nothing less than the defense of man. Hitler's Germany, today's political terrorists and the explosion of street crime everywhere that usurps the place of constructive news in our papers tempt us to think man merely a destructive beast out for blood. The teacher of the humanities must show how profound, how rich, how marvellous has been, and still is, the expression of the human spirit through the ages. Perhaps it is King Alfred directing his school of translators to bring learning and piety to the Anglo-Saxons; perhaps it is Plato giving order to the universe in the *Timaeus*; perhaps it is King Lear saying, "Pray you now, forget and forgive"; perhaps it is Leonard Rose playing Dvořák's cello concerto; perhaps it is Bronowski recording the *Ascent of Man*—the knowledge and experience of these measures of what man has achieved are necessary to keep youth's expectation of human achievement pitched high. He cannot despair of man, who has done so much. With what else can man fortify his spirit against the danger of nuclear contamination of the race or against eternal hatreds of clan for clan and eternal injustice of the strong against the weak? Only by holding steadfastly before himself evidences of man's ability to live richly in a dangerous world, and it is the preeminent duty of teachers to present these evidences with power, with conviction. I am not arguing for a view of man that denies his failures — and they have been many — but since it takes so little search just now

106

to find them, it is necessary to hit the high points in his history.

When we look closely at the failures, the very knowledge of how numerous they have been helps to keep our courage up. If the parents of the disruptive students of the sixties had realized that students began to behave decently only in this century, that in the Middle Ages they pillaged, beat up their enemies, sometimes laid siege to a whole town; that even in the calm days of Queen Victoria, at least in this country, they took delight in overturning street cars or small buildings, looting, and generally raising hell, perhaps they would not have utterly despaired of education and of their own offspring. I am not condoning violence. I am only saying that a knowledge of its having been with us always sometimes keeps us from despair. Man is capable of greatness and he is also capable of bestiality. Hitler's attempted extermination of the Jews will never cease to appall us, but it is not unique. We do not need to invoke Genghis Khan's bloody march across Asia to find parallels. Even in our western culture the Jews have been expelled from every nation many times over. The Moriscos were cruelly driven out of Spain and turned literally into galley slaves. The most Christian crusaders in the name of religion exterminated every Moslem they could lay hands on. These are trite observations, but when so many students know so little history it is worthwhile to remind them of these things. They are prone to despair.

But in the end the total effect of his education should be to make the student feel himself a part of humanity's finest achievements, and this he will not feel if the teacher talks down to him. The instructor should talk up to him, pitch his expectations higher than he thinks his students can reach, and often they will surprise him by reaching them.

What changes would I like to see in higher education? First, I would like society to narrow its demands on colleges and universities. I am by no means sure that slum clearance, for example, is best planned and executed by academics. Let municipalities develop their own experts and take the responsibility for making their plans work. If these outside demands were diminished we would not need the vast array of administrative officers, and these able men and women could either enter the mainstream of education or offer leadership to enterprises outside the university or college. Think of the money that would be saved!

A corollary to this change might be better relations between faculty and administration. It is one of the scars on the educational body that both distrust each other all too often, a distrust that would usually vanish if there were time and patience on both sides to understand the position of the other. The faculty feel that they are the university, that all too much money goes into projecting a good image in the community, money that might better go to laboratories and libraries. They have little patience with all the red tape demanded in a complex educational system and all too little appreciation of the patient deans and sub-deans that deal with it. The administration often looks on the subject-centered individuals that stand in the way of efficiency and experimentation as poor team members and would often like to rule them by fiat. To be sure, the faculty often needs a larger view of university well-being, and the administration more understanding of the passionate clinging by the faculty to what they conceive as standards that result from deep involvement with learning. Deans and presidents look at Professor X, unproductive yet protected by tenure, and they would like to get rid of him. Sometimes they are right, but he was not given tenure without their consent. And usually, if he is really incompetent, they could fire him with impunity if they took the trouble to clear the matter with the local chapter of A.A.U.P. I think that in many cases administrative officers should concern themselves more deeply in what is actually taught and learned in the university, and that the faculty should usually welcome that concern and not regard it as an invasion by the enemy. Sometimes there are departmental matters that cannot be settled by the department alone.

On the demands that society makes there is one about which I feel passionately and know little. It should not demand professional athletic entertainment from colleges and universities. Athletics should be de-professionalized and returned to its place as a regular part of education. If the public cannot be entertained by athletic contests between students whose primary interest is in the classroom and not the football field, let them watch the

Dorothy B. Loomis

Green Bay Packers and all the other honest professionals. To offer them professional college teams under the guise of students playing for fun is basically dishonest and an educational disgrace. Again, think of the money that would be saved, and, more important, the educations. For the number of students who can play on any of the Big League teams and still do a good job as students is minimal.

To return to the faculty's activities, the structure of the curriculum is, as always, of current interest. Curricular changing is the occupational disease of teachers. Since the vogue just now is "Return to Basics" I will say little about it except that I think students need considerably more direction in shaping their education than they have recently had, and that it is the faculty's responsibility to provide that direction, giving a student just as much control over the shape of his education as he is able to take, but insisting on a framework that will insure a humanistic education and not mere forays into the fringes of knowledge.

And now there is a change that I would like to see take place in faculty loyalties. For the past twenty or twenty-five years teachers have tended to feel considerably more loyalty to their branch of learning than to the institution where they exercise their skills. I would not for a moment loosen that tie nor diminish the pleasure and stimulation we have all got from meeting scholars in our field from many institutions. This is valuable and necessary. But I would plead for closer ties to college or university than now exist, for a feeling of responsibility to it which would prevent the casual hopping from one place to another that disrupts continuity and destroys the character of an institution. A student attending a university because he wishes to study under Professor A should have a reasonable expectation of finding him there. Recently it has been a mark of status to receive many invitations from many institutions to come and be a visiting professor for a year, and valuable members have yielded to this seduction even when it came from institutions no better than nor even as good as their own. To a limited degree this change of scene has value for both teacher and institution, but it should be held within reasonable bounds, and before accepting these invitations a teacher should ask himself, "What will happen to my own classes and to my own students?"

109

Confronting Crisis

The weakening of the feeling of responsibility to institutions is related to another matter, and that is money. Before Sputnik, learned and able teachers received salaries lower than did the garbage collectors in Chicago. There was wide lamentation about it, but little was done, simply because society paid the lowest price possible for education and was able to. Teachers entered the profession not to make money, for that was impossible, but because they wanted to teach. After Sputnik the public placed a much higher value on learning and began to be willing to pay for it, so that now a young man entering the profession no longer has to choose between teaching and properly clothing his children. To be sure there are exceptions, but by and large teaching now pays a living wage. This is not altogether a gain for the profession, because where formerly it attracted mainly those who wanted to study and to teach, now, alas, there is a fair number of young people on the make who want both the status and the money the profession now supplies, and they will never make good teachers. I do not want to go back to the starvation days, but I would urge department chairmen and deans to take a stern look at the applying assistant professor — there are no instructors any more — and develop a test for purity of motive.

I have talked as if this profession were a simon-pure one, as if it did not have its drudgery and its drones. It has plenty of both and is such hard work that nobody would endure it who did not find its rewards far beyond its demands. I have been trying to talk about good teachers and well ordered institutions. Even with its flaws it is such a profession that anyone who has spent a life in it can ask no better gift of fortune.

Father **Paul Barrus**, native Iowan, received his B.A. in English and Latin from Drake University, where he was named to Phi Beta Kappa. Later he obtained the M.A. in Latin from Drake, and, after serving in the army during World War II, he returned to his native state where he was awarded the Ph.D. in English and Latin from State University of Iowa. He taught both at Drake and Iowa State before coming to East Texas State University, Commerce, in 1952. Soon after retirement as Head of the English Department, by a special dispensation from Pope John Paul I he was ordained priest.

Paul W. Barrus

The Furnished Mind

It has been said that the unexamined life is not worth living, for without spiritual and intellectual reflection, evaluation, and the identification of priorities our brief sojourn on this planet is liable to become a frantic pursuit of what for the moment is dubbed happiness — a nonchalant, almost mindless euphoria buttressed with slogans extolling the so-called positive attitude toward the daily encounters, devotion to the creed of *carpe diem*, and a naive reliance on what is called education — all this despite the violence that turns newspapers into horror sheets, the ephemeral adoration of fads and fancies, and especially the loud acclaim given to schools and colleges that annually produce hordes of young Americans who are impervious to the written word and unable to produce a coherent sentence. How long can we continue to ignore the distortion and prostitution of man's unique and crowning glory, the patient, serious, disciplined, cultivation of the intellect? It is time to pause — to pay homage and grant recognition to this precious endowment upon which our future depends.

In the words of a famous American, it is altogether fitting and proper that we should do this, for there are manifold forces at work in the world engaged in ruthless warfare against the

113

things of the mind and spirit. Our ears are battered and our eyes sated with the blandishments of sense and the allure of the merely transient. One turns on his radio or television to the caterwauling of an unquiet soul, who, incidentally, is highly remunerated for his wailing and bellowing about some visceral disturbance that he has labeled love. Encroaching upon the fresh green of our Texas landscape, a billboard hysterically exhorts us to flee from the ostracism that will surely be ours without a surefire deodorant designed not only to obliterate offensive body odors but also to act as a delicate aphrodisiac. From another wayside entreaty, a sylphlike siren with apparently few, if any, inhibitions models what in less unbuttoned days were known as "unmentionables." Still another assures us that sufficient intake of a particular brand of firewater will metamorphose us into Adonises — young, robust, sophisticated, and devastatingly "cool."

Our newsstands are no mean factors on the catering to raw sensation, though, under the genteel guise of "literature," their tactics are somewhat less blatant. On magazine covers, however, one notes a preoccupation, almost an obsession, with nakedness, which probably is not entirely motivated by devotion to the beauty of the human form. In secluded sections of many bookstores, one may enjoy vicarious orgies without the inconvenience of travel and free from the watchful eyes of neighbors.

I do not wish to assume the mantle of a rabid reformer, the dour countenance of a narrow-minded prude, or the fretful faultfinding of a frustrated pedagogue. It seems to me that any thoughtful person must pause — that he must in all seriousness propound to himself this question: Is this apparent dedication to the cheap, the tawdry, the pathetically temporary an index to the values of our people? This crude exhibitionism, this pellmell scramble for the nervous kicks of debased amusement or the lethal euphoria of drugs, this blind worship of the latest sly slogan, this scrapping of the lessons of centuries of human experience. Must our yardstick of excellence be "It turns me on"?

Perhaps the root of our dilemma lies in a philosophy that has unfortunately sprung up with and accompanied the amazing conquest of natural forces which has been the glory — and may

114

be the Nemesis — of our generation. I refer to the philosophy of expediency, the belief that the ends justify any means, though these ends may never have been weighed and evaluated in the light of the experience of the race. Insidiously, this pattern of thought has insinuated itself into diverse areas of American life, including that of education.

The problem of the schools has been aggravated by the American dedication to the proposition that a free education is the birthright and salvation of all our youth. To this concept we have been committed since the days of the Founding Fathers; it is one of our most cherished ideals. As a result of our mode of implementing this conviction, we find today that our public schools enroll many uninterested, unprepared, semi-illiterate, and rebellious students. And, mistaking crowds for zeal, size for quality, and palatial appointments for attainment, we complacently assure ourselves that our great nation "leads the world in education." Yet we must not be deluded. "A house builded on sands cannot stand." A mighty educational system, however majestic and impressive its facade, is a hollow tomb — a tomb of the intellect — if its procedures and policies are governed primarily by unexamined ends snatched from the flux of the transient and the ephemeral.

The fruit of the development of the intellect is a furnished mind, and the role of the school is the definition and promulgation of those experiences which will produce that sort of mind. Here ends must be scrutinized for their intrinsic validity; they must not be determined by the loudest advertiser, the most cunning self-seeker or the most persuasive purveyor of gadgetry. The criterion for the identification of the intrinsic validity of ends is the extent to which they orient man into this mysterious universe in which, during his brief adventure into consciousness that we call human life, he finds himself. The nature of this orientation — let it never be forgotten — is twofold: adjustment to his physical environment and at-homeness in the world of ideas — pure ideas — to which his God given intellect alone gives him access. To neglect the first of these is to render man helpless in the face of natural forces; to curtail the second is to make him less than human. It is a deplorable fact that contemporary thinking is centered almost wholly upon the first of these

115

orientations, that is, adjustment to the material world. It has been said that a poll of students would probably reveal that so-called social prestige and success in terms of money are the prime motivators of their matriculation in institutions of higher learning. These goals are not to be held in lofty contempt, but it is a tragic mistake to ascribe to them paramount, if not exclusive, significance. Unaccompanied by the uniquely human and infinitely precious capacity for ideation, they become, in the words of St. Paul, as "sounding brass and a tinkling cymbal."

In the days of confusion when men cry "lo here" and "lo there," it is encouraging to observe that some have not been turned aside from their high purpose. Overcoming the natural indolence that impedes all of us and putting first things first, they have nurtured the flame of intellectual curiosity, which is their peculiarly human heritage. And in so doing they have enriched themselves for all the days to come.

There is no more poignant human tragedy than to approach maturity with an unfurnished mind, a mind that has no resources in itself, a mind that has depended for its sustenance upon passing fads and physical prowess. When I was a child in a small town, I used to wonder about the rows of older men who sat, day after day, in the courthouse yard, staring dully into space or forever whittling. They had come to the evening of life with unfurnished minds. Their lackluster eyes looked out upon a world that was strange — alien — for the infirmities of age and the fading of passion had divorced them from the only activities they knew. Throughout the long midwestern summer days, they sat waiting, waiting. Now, when I return home for vacation, another generation I see in the courthouse yard — still waiting.

In contrast with the pathetic figures was an old gentleman named Mr. Cooper. We children at school knew him well, for each year on Lincoln's birthday he came to tell us a story, the story of Gettysburg, where he, a Federal soldier, watched with a lump in his throat the magnificent charge of Pickett's forces, rightly called the flower of the South, as they swept up the ridge. We always looked for him at the public library, where we scurried after classes, for he was almost always there. I can see him yet, sitting by the great window that looked out upon Main Street, the light of the low winter sun illuminating his fine old

face. We school children involuntarily softened our footsteps
and spoke in whispers. The old man was rapt in his reading. He
was alive and eternally young in the world of ideas. Throughout
the long years, he had been busy furnishing his mind.

Maxwell Henry Goldberg was born in Malden, Massachusetts, October 22, 1907. Educated at the University of Massachusetts and Yale, he is threefold emeritus: Commonwealth Professor of the Humanities, University of Massachusetts; Professor of Humanities and English, Pennsylvania State University; and Distinguished Professor of Humanities and Literature, Converse College, South Carolina. A humanist, his research interests include public broadcasting, career education, technological change, futuristics, blindness research, telic man, cybernation, automation, and human values.

Maxwell H. Goldberg

The Lights Men Live By

Commencement Day is a time both of endings and beginnings. It stirs regrets for opportunities missed. It evokes nostalgia for happy times, remembrance of things past. It throbs with anticipatory excitement, triggers even some seismic tremors, misgivings about the unknown future.

At such a time, it is well to look both backward and forward. As Emerson said, "The days are made on a loom whereof the warp and woof are past and future time." Let us attend to such weaving today. Let us form — in understanding hearts — an assessment of the psychic stock, the psychic reserves our graduates may have accumulated to strengthen them as wayfarers into the future. This is to practice the master art of humane learning, the projective design-making, goal-seeking art of life itself.

In a recent press article a father presented his thoughts at Commencement time. Believing "them to be like those of thousands of other parents this month," he did just the sort of weaving backward and forward in time that I have suggested. He did so in connection with his own daughter's graduation. As he watched his daughter walk across the stage to receive her diploma, it was hard to ignore the memories. "Could this be the

119

Confronting Crisis

same girl we worried about at fifteen, when she carried cigarets in her purse, the same girl who now may ask a friend, 'What right do you have to pollute my air without my permission?' " Already, what a contrast! Already "so much tragedy in so short a life": assassination in American public life, visiting her closest girl friend dying of cancer at eighteen, spending days at the hospital, holding her hand to help ease the pain, occasionally leaving to place a rose on the altar of a nearby church, the death of her younger sister after a brave battle against a pernicious disease.

The father had the same question that has been asked since the Greeks: What causes one person to crumble and another to strengthen under such personal blows?

When I review my own search for an answer to this question, I find an extraordinary contrast between the deplored generation gap claimed for us in the 1970s and the enriching and sustaining realities of my past experiences. Far from finding unbridgeable gaps between me and the once younger generation and the then older generation (father and son, teacher and student), I found wide and life giving channels of interchange and communication. By these mutually respecting intergenerational streams, I was bathed in enriching nutrients, and I feel myself, still, to be, thereby, the stronger person.

I wish now to share some of these riches, drawn from the realms of gold in poetry — literature, history, philosphy and the arts — and riches drawn no less from the very experiences of living itself.

What causes one person to crumble and another to strengthen under personal blows? the father asked. The nineteenth century poet Matthew Arnold found one answer in the words of Homer: "For an enduring heart have the gods given to man." Arnold used this as a talisman to ward off the doubt and the melancholy that bred about his heart. I, too, have found, in this Homeric utterance, a sort of talisman. I am reminded of the words of that large-hearted man and sensitive poet who came from Kentucky to Amherst in the 1920s, becoming my dear friend. To a volume of his finely wrought lyrics, he gave the title *Spell Against Time.* For me the Homeric touchstone, "For an enduring heart have the gods given to man," has become again and again, such a "spell against time."

Among the experiences that have exercised such a spell for me, that have given me the heart to endure, are those occasioned by my own past teachers, friends, and mentors in that same town of Amherst. Some were poets. One of them exclaimed: "This is their acre. Here the bright word fell." It was David Morton himself who so declared. After the lapse of some thirty years, the poems that he wrote in the deepening darkness of the Second World War, when the lights were going out again, not only all over Europe, but over the rest of the world, these poems read again now, are still extraordinarily moving. They signal across the years to the present. They become radiant with a civilizing light that gives eternal rebuke to the blinding brightness of that first atomic bomb exploded over the sandy wastes of Los Alamos. The poet's light gives such rebuke to that mordant mushroom cloud whose glare, as one of its chief creators, Dr. Oppenheimer, described it, was "brighter than the light of a thousand suns."

What, in the face of such ghastly flares and holocausts, were the humanizing lights that David Morton celebrated? As in his prose and the world of action, so in his verse and the images of the poet. Pity and love, these were the first two of the pieties David Morton named in his poem "Notation for the Record." These, together with "learning hardly won," says the poet, are the "flickering lights men live by in the dark": The light of pity, the light of love.

Another poet who for many years lived in Amherst held these up as lights for me to live by. He was Robert Frost. Some critics have called him "tough minded." Tough minded he appeared to the tough talking steelworkers who, years later, became my students in an experimental program on knowing human values through the study of poetry.

I think now of how these unlettered but often sensitive men responded to the light in Frost's "The Death of the Hired Man." This poetic illumination was like the lamplight itself in the farmhouse where, as the poem has it, the case is poignantly made for the understanding heart. It is the light struck from the flint of the husband's practical, commonsensical, legalistic definition of home. (His name is Warren — itself suggesting warranty.) "Home," he brusquely says, "is the place where, when you have to go there, / They have to take you in." This is compassionately sublimated in the gently chiding, fond, pleading reply of the wife, significantly named Mary: "I should have called it / Something you somehow haven't to deserve."

This is a hard lesson for Warren, the farm manager, the man of the house, to learn. But learn it he does, with death and the life-enhancing Mary as his teachers. He learns the lesson of the unearned increment that comes from the transmuting elements of pity and love — compassion. This is truly fitting to our common humanity and our common plight, to what we fashionably intellectualize as the "human condition," the "human situation," or the "human predicament." And it is the light of compassion which Frost helped me slowly learn to live by, especially to redeem the dark.

People have been taking out their envy and spite on one of the greatest poets of our century. Seizing upon his self-revealed, all too evident, and all too human weaknesses, they have tried to make a heartless monster of Robert Frost. I have a different picture of this man. I remember, especially, one rainy Sunday afternoon in autumn, when I stopped by to see him in the Amherst quarters reserved for him at the Lord Jeffrey Inn. My purpose was to extend an invitation for him to speak at a conference on Industry and the Liberal Arts that I was arranging, and that was to be held at the recently dedicated Corning Glass Center. He accepted the invitation. My business being done, I was about to leave. "What's your rush?" he asked. "I don't have to be anywhere until five. It's only two-thirty now. Stay awhile." So I stayed, and the poet talked. He talked of his feelings about his father, his mother, his daughter. He talked of his son, who had committed suicide. Concerning him, a shrewish reviewer in the *New York Times Book Review* alleged that Frost exhibited, to the full, his inhuman callousness, his self-centered and self-seeking hardness of heart.

What a contrast with what Robert Frost himself told me of this tragic event. "That was one time," Frost said, in a tone of infinite regret and infinite sadness, "that was one time, when all my rhetoric and all my eloquence failed." (He pronounced that "all" in his characteristic drawl; and his voice, in the Shakespearean phrase, had "a dying fall.")

Then I knew how misleading was the stereotypic picture of Robert Frost as just a soft, sentimental nature poet, or that other one of him as just a cracker barrel wit and humorist. I knew that Robert Frost's muse was really a tragic muse. I recalled that a volume of Greek tragedies was always close by him, and that it accompanied him on his many trips. So at heart, to use Professor Richard Sewall's telling concept, Frost's was a tragic vision of life. It was compounded heavily of those tragic emotions, terror and pity. The light Frost shed for me was the somber tragic light.

I could thus better understand what Frost means when he describes a poem as a "stay against confusion," or again as a means of "containing our own chaos." Or when, in that favorite poem of mine, "West-Running Brook," he describes existence as "the universal cataract of death." Yet he points to one white wave that forever rides the black waters which "spend to nothingness." He notes what some would call the "anti-entropic" resistance of that one white wave, not gaining but not losing, "always raising a little, sending up a little."

Both David Morton and Robert Frost, in those Amherst days, held in warm and reciprocated regard a third man of poetic mind and heart. He lived in Amherst for all too brief a time, a year at the most, but he likewise gave me lights to live by. He was my father; and through the barriers of language and difference in culture, the other Amherst poets let him know they welcomed him, as a kindred spirit, to their republic of letters. When I try to suggest their sentiments for my father, I think of what has been said concerning Dr. Frank Graham: "I have a piety for that man." This was how people felt about my father. He was in the twilight of his own life, in the almost darkness rather, for in the state records office he was technically classified as "blind." Yet he managed to go on with his beloved writing, to keep his mind from going stagnant, "to keep his brain sharp," he would say. In his eighties, he still wrote poems to spring and the spirit of youthful love. He still managed to hold something of youth in his heart. He still commanded the bright lexicon which, in the play, Cardinal Richelieu declared to be the prerogative of youth.

In a memorable Day of Atonement service, my good friend,

Confronting Crisis

Rabbi William J. Broude, once declared: "The spirit of man is the candle of the Lord, and the flame of a candle burns most brightly when the air is still." My father was such a candle of the Lord, and he was an agent of light, all the more effective for burning as a candle most brightly, when the air was still. He had an unshakeable faith in the residual goodness of man, as of life itself. Nor was this, for him, a mere phrase. It was felt deeply and as a motivating conviction. Cleanth Brooks has said of William Faulkner that he was profoundly Christian, that there was an essential Christianity in the very marrow of his bones. So we might say of the conviction, for David Morton and my father, of the indomitable goodness of man. It was something in the very marrow of their bones.

Let me give one instance of the powerful will to faith and hope that animated my gentle-seeming father, and the effectiveness with which he thus sparked hope in us of the younger generation. The happening occurred during the dark days already mentioned, of the Second World War, when we found ourselves the allies of the Russians. It was at the time of the siege of Stalingrad; and things looked very bad for the allies.

My father was to undergo surgery; and this was all the more serious because of his age. The evening before, we children had come to the hospital for what, we feared, might be a lasting farewell. We could not conceal our fear, and my father heard it in our voices. Soon the nurse told us it was time to leave. We moved toward the door. But my father called me back. I thought: it must be some very serious last-minute request or instruction. When I got close to him, he looked up at me with a smile, and asked in Yiddish: "*Mein Suhn! Wie hält es mit Stalingrad?*"

This is very hard to translate. The difficult, and pivotal, word is *hält*. This word simultaneously makes the question ask two things. First: My son, how stands it with Stalingrad? (That is, in English idiom, how goes it with Stalingrad?) Second: My son, does Stalingrad still stand? (That is: Does Stalingrad still hold out?) My reply, in mingled astonishment and relief, was: "Stalingrad still stands!"

"Good!" my father said. He looked up at me. There was light in his glance. "Good!" He waved to me in a gesture both of

124

Maxwell H. Goldberg

affectionate dismissal and of benediction: "Good — Now go!"
Like that one word, *hält,* my father's "good" and his
gesture had double meaning. They meant, first: "Look, my son:
you may have written me off; but I haven't signed off yet! I'm
still part of life, and I'm still concerned about the future." They
meant, also: "Take heart, my son. The present moment may
seem terribly threatening. But it will pass. You must see it in the
light of time and history. That way, you reduce it to proper scale.
Then the moment can no longer tyrannize over you."

Once — in the years of that terrible disaster to all mankind
— the universal catastrophe of Hitler and the Holocaust, when I
came to see my father at this little place in the country — his
"farm" he called it, I found him — of all things — planting apple
seedlings. I playfully taxed him with this. He was quite old, after
all; and even an early maturing of the trees was some years away.

"Why are you doing this? You won't reap the harvest."

"Why am I doing this?" echoed my father. "You don't
know?"—

"No."

"Don't you see, my son? It's quite simple. This is my answer
to Hitler."

It was not until enough years had gone by to bring ample
harvest from those trees that I fully understood my father's simple reply. This is my answer to Hitler.

The Hitlers of the world might come and go. More than six
million of my father's fellow Jews and hundreds of thousands of
other innocent human beings might go to feed the extermination
furnaces and the gas chambers of the Hitlerians of the world. But
so long as those who could do so kept facing toward the future,
and kept proving their faith in the future by making life-
enhancing investments in it, of which they themselves might
never reap the profits, so long was man indomitable.

Many times since, through magnification of my own — in
my self-pitying view — sorry plight, when I have found myself
threatened with failure of nerve, I have asked myself: *Wie hält es
mit Stalingrad?* The lights I live by have not flickered quite so fit-
fully. I have renewed heart.

A quiet man, my father, burning with the quiet flame of a
candle. Yet an extraordinary force for faith in the long-range

125

power of the human spirit. In his unpretentious and unsung way, he fulfilled the imperative that Albert Camus enjoined upon us in his speech of acceptance of the Nobel award: "While we are men, we cope." He demonstrated the Homeric dictum: "For an enduring heart have the gods given to man."

My theme bears a paradox and holds a double motif. "Our being," says Carlyle, "is made up of Light and Darkness, the Light resting on the Darkness and balancing it." So with my present theme. It is a counterpoint. Its warp is darkness, its weft is light. Let the light stand out.

I recall that ardent lover of the humanities, of the arts and liberal learning, the blind poet Milton. I recall that other blind poet to whom Milton felt so close to kinship, Homer. Let us be prepared, with them, to see our way through darkness. But let us, as does Milton, be all the readier to rejoice in the light. May all of us walk together in the light of that liberal learning which it is our joyous privilege to serve and which, noblesse oblige, in turn, so richly and variously may serve us. It is a light for us and for our lives across the years, wherever we live, move, and have our being.

Waldo Forest NcNeir, a native Texan, born in Houston,
September 13, 1908, attended Rice University and the University
of North Carolina, where he was granted the Ph.D. He has been
a Fulbright lecturer at the University of Marburg and also at the
University of Muenster. After more than a decade of teaching at
Louisiana State University, he moved to the University of
Oregon where he continued his Renaissance studies in
Shakespeare and Spenser. "My essay," he writes, "is frankly
autobiographical. I think that my experiences may, in some
sense, define the humanities."

Waldo F. McNeir

A Separate Peace

A sort of manifest destiny impelled me to become an English teacher. When I was a child in Houston, my bookish though blind grandmother, who was "of infinite remembrance" and had the gift of story telling, enthralled me and other neighborhood kids with Walter Scott from *Guy Mannering* to *Woodstock*, Charles Reade's *The Cloister and the Hearth*, and Dickens from *Oliver Twist* to *A Tale of Two Cities*. My father had received the same kind of tutoring from her, as he says in his autobiography, *Forest McNeir of Texas*. My parents encouraged me to read aloud to them the Martian tales of Edgar Rice Burroughs, fantasies more realistic than the confused primitivism of the Tarzan books. When we played "Knights of the Round Table," a game I made up after reading *Tales of King Arthur*, I was Lancelot and the little girl across the street, on whom I had a crush, was Guinevere. Before my teens, while the war to "make the world safe for democracy" was in progress, I had romanticized the battles of the Civil War into confederate victories, with the help of John Esten Cooke and the articles and colored maps in the eleventh edition of the *Encyclopedia Britannica*.

This privileged childhood stimulated the development of initiative and imagination. South End Junior High School, a

129

beautiful building then, and heterogeneous Central High School, long since demolished, were at best semi-benevolent. Bearing out Alfred Adler's concept of adolescence as a social phenomenon, youngsters sought their own level in small cliques, each with its peculiar shibboleths and taboos. Some fought to get into the Mickey Mouse courses of "favorite" teachers, who were notoriously the least competent; but somehow I managed to study under a few capable ones. There was competition for grades and the popularity that came with elective office, almost equally insignificant as indicators of later academic achievement. We knew that "Johnny couldn't read" long before the educationists discovered it, but we knew that we could read; and thus began the separation of blockheads from smart alecks that became more acute in college.

Rice Institute (now a fine university) in 1925 had a provincial student body characterized by a debilitating narrow mindedness, and a few luminaries on its faculty imported from Ivy League schools or from Europe to teach culture to local hobbledehoys. Luckily, in my freshman year I discovered George Williams, a young Texan and Teaching Assistant in the English department who was an inspiring teacher, wise in his large heartedness, his unfailing considerateness, and his rigorous expectations of his students. Although I could write pretty well, as a fine stylist himself he insisted that I write better. He has remained my most trusted counselor and friend for more than fifty years.

As a town boy, I was also lucky to find *compadres* among my classmates from San Antonio, Galveston, Dallas, and other "foreign" places. We were considered radicals by the dilettantes (later known as playboys) and the jocks, because we rejected William Jennings Bryan as an interpreter of the Bible, talked glibly about Darwin's theory of natural selection without understanding it, maintained that poetry was superior to petroleum engineering, and had the temerity to establish *The Raven*, a mildly satirical little mag which so enraged the campus citizenry that it was roasted in the yearbook, *The Campanile*.

I did my first teaching at Rice the year after my graduation. Grading freshman themes forced me to become a proficient, but not infallible, speller. I tried to follow the example of George

Waldo F. McNeir

Williams; I succeeded only in upholding his high standards, but without his graciousness. Young teachers are harder graders than older teachers. I enjoyed having power over a bunch of people who didn't know something that I knew, whether it was when to use a semicolon or the identity of Epictetus, and I had a compulsion for setting people straight. Not that I did it right, but that was the urge. Perhaps I got this from the eminent eighteenth-century scholar, Alan Dougald McKillop, a rather dour figure who told me that I'd have to like the novels of Jane Austen, which I was pretending to dislike, in order to pass his course. His most enthusiastic sign of approbation on an A-plus paper was a hen scratch in the margin: "I think you have a point here." Or I may have picked it up from the distinguished historian, Floyd Lear, in his dogmatic but enormously informative lectures on European civilization in the Middle Ages. A novice teacher imitates a number of models before he finds his own style.

As a graduate student at the University of North Carolina in Chapel Hill, I found many different models among my professors, some to be imitated for a while, others to be forever avoided. My own revered mentor, the medievalist George Raleigh Coffman, was a kindly, modest man of deep learning; but his lectures were painfully disjointed, punctuated by blurts and pauses, ejaculated with effort in spasmodic sentences. I thought his shyness made him seem unsure of himself. In contrast, the authority on Shakespeare and Milton, George Coffin Taylor, was confident and high strung in his seemingly extemporaneous manner, rattling off quotations from *Hamlet* or *Paradise Lost*; but he was extremely disorganized as he plucked lecture notes written on the backs of soiled envelopes from the side pockets of his rumpled suit, and threw these scraps of paper about with fine abandon. His antics were popular with many students, but they set my teeth on edge. For the rest, the English faculty included teachers that we called: the poisonous Pekinese/great papa bear/the unworried Abe Lincoln/the dullard/the lady-like Victorian/stock broker/the pink porker/the little bald headed nincompoop — a galaxy of disrespectful monikers such as students since the time of the Wandering Scholars have pinned on their profs.

131

Confronting Crisis

I was fortunate in my teaching career that spanned forty-five years to serve at two universities in the Southwest (Rice and North Texas State), two in the South (North Carolina and LSU), one in the Middle West (Chicago), and one in the Pacific Northwest (Oregon). Moreover, I spent four years as an officer in the Navy, seeing some action, as well as some famous sights, in both Western and Eastern hemispheres during World War II, the one "to free the world from the threat of Fascism," and the last war that united this country in a common cause. Even during this non-academic interlude it was necessary for me to be a teacher, and in firm control. In addition, I have three times been a Fulbright Lecturer in Germany, twice at the University of Marburg, once at the University of Muenster. Travel to other countries is broadening, as Beowulf learned. It is the best antidote to provincialism, as Montaigne pointed out. Domestic and foreign travel keep a teacher's mind from getting stuck in the same groove. Both should be compulsory for prospective teachers.

At North Carolina I played a few tricks on my Tar Heel freshmen, who were loaded with Southern gentility, such as offering them a class cut if all of them could write the alphabet in correct sequence. Not all of them could. I was more sedate with the sophomores to whom I disclosed some of the realms of gold in a survey of English literature. A few of these students were as able as any undergraduates I have ever met, Phi Beta Kappas in the making.

At that time I realized with something of a shock that I could stimulate the best and the brightest students and I could occasionally reach and help the mediocre students, but I could do nothing with the poorest students who were in greatest need of any help they could get. I brooded over this as I watched with envy as some of my lowly peers blossomed into great favorites with the unendowed, including the intellectual basket cases. My failure with these was especially upsetting during the weekly huddles of the Freshman English staff, at which "the unworried Abe Lincoln" presided, and much cant was rehearsed about "meeting the students at their own level." Why couldn't we ask them to meet us on the university level for which they had theoretically been prepared? As in most cases of shilly-shallying over educational policy, sufficient to the time is the nonsense thereof. So it was revealed early that I could not suffer fools gladly. I was of a temperament that appealed to excellent students and good students, but not very much to C students, and not at all to students outside the pale.

As a full-fledged Ph.D. with a dissertation on Robert Greene and as an unfledged Assistant Professor, I went to North Texas State; the students there in those days, with few exceptions, seemed less ambitious and more content to be third-raters than those at Rice or North Carolina. Without striving on the part of some students, there can be little excitement. The faculty, too, seemed oppressed by their own passivity. Yet the unassuming dignity of Floyd Stovall, the Whitman scholar, and that of Arthur Sampley, the Shakespeare scholar and esteemed poet, were noble attributes.

After the war years I received a *Beruf*, as German academicians say, to the College then riding high at the University of Chicago, the brain child of Robert Maynard Hutchins and his sidekick Mortimer Adler. Their theory was that the undergraduate college, staffed by a faculty of competent generalists, should educate students in the ideas and disciplines of the humanities, science, and social science that are the components of human culture, all of these enclosed in a completely required curriculum. The "Great Books" program was a spin-off. It was a sound theory. How sound we see in the return, led by Harvard, to a hardware core of knowledge essential to produce educated people, after decades of software electives (Elementary Baton Twirling, Intermediate Baking, and Advanced Breathing) within specialized "majors" and "minors" have educated nobody.

A rarefied intellectual atmosphere prevailed at Chicago, a heady feeling that students and faculty were pursuing the life of the mind. A boy and a girl walking hand in hand on the Midway campus were discussing Plato and Aristotle, or Ptolemy and Copernicus, or Gibbon and Burke — to all of whom they had been exposed. Such students were a luxury to teach, although little interaction with them was possible. The Whiz Kids, conceited about their sky high I.Q.s, let themselves be told what to think and how to think about it. They were spoon-fed on a rich but pre-digested diet. When, as a generalist, I had to help to plan, design, and put together texts for use in Composition, Humanities, and History courses — no published texts were good enough, so we published our own — it was difficult to think of myself as a specialist in English Renaissance literature.

Every utopia has dystopian aspects. The latter were centered in weekly staff meetings, ostensibly on how to present the stupendous reading assignments in a fairly uniform manner. In actuality these sessions were like war games, bouts of fierce one-upmanship in which everybody was determined to display his own clever *aperçus*. The "completely required curriculum" was constantly being revamped, as if the preservation of culture rested on our decisions. The result would have delighted Heraclitus, showing that all things exist in a state of flux, that only change is permanent. Innovation for its own sake was a natural law of the College. To me, after three years of tinkering, our deliberations seemed as trivial as the Cake Bakers' War of Rabelais.

I was confident that I would find at Louisiana State University a more traditional kind of higher education. Indeed it was, the old fashioned Southern fried variety in which Jim Crow, not innovation, was the abiding principle. The Supreme Court decision of 1954 in *Brown v. Board of Education* had been heard but unheeded along the bayous. Now I became the innovator, and moreover a dangerous incendiary, one who wanted to "destroy our Southern heritage," or "betray our Southern way of life." I became a charter member and then President of the Louisiana affiliate of the ACLU, taking public stands for the heresies of integrated education and civil rights for Negroes. This was nearly ten years before the sit-ins, the civil rights marches, and the court victories of the 1960s dragged a recalcitrant South, still protesting, into the American main stream.

The light that blazed in the 1960s was only a flicker in the 1950s. How did the students at LSU react to the encroachment of social change? How did the faculty react? My undergraduates perceptibly stiffened; my graduate students brightened. My young colleagues talked freely, and in some of them, I thought, lay the hopes of the New South. My elders, senior professors and administrators with vested interests in the status quo, opposed automatically any social change. "Our Nigras are happy," one of them told me. "They don't want civil rights, wouldn't know what to do with 'em. Best to let sleeping dogs lie." He was oblivious to the attitude he had revealed.

At this juncture the perennially inept Louisiana state legislature convened, breathing defiance of federal intervention in forcing two elementary schools in New Orleans to admit a few black children, threatening to secede from the Union again, rehashing the doctrine of nullification (shade of John C. Calhoun), and creating a carnival by passing unanimously a resolution to investigate me, with an appropriation of $25,000 of taxpayers' money, for Communist leanings. When I exercised my rights as a citizen and wrote to my state representatives urging them to act like enlightened statesmen, or to assume a virtue if they had it not, my letters were made public, and the hurricane that followed blew away all semblance of reason.

The President of LSU, Lieutenant General (ret.) Troy Middleton, seemed a strong and unruffled executive, not at all in the stereotyped mold of a military tyrant. Like a good soldier, however, he carried out the orders of the Board of Supervisors, who took their orders from the state legislature. To his credit, the General (nobody called him "President") had outfaced a joint session of the legislature two years before when he told the law makers that at LSU academic freedom was protected. Now things were different. The General came under tremendous political pressure from many unreconstructed Rebels — those whose grandfathers had not surrendered at Appomattox, others to whom states rights were worth a new crusade, and red necks who turned apoplectic at the mention of "Washin'tun." Not far ahead were "Impeach Earl Warren" billboards. The legislature threatened to withhold the entire university budget unless I was fired. My staunchest supporters agreed that I wasn't worth that much.

Yet the General disappointed me when he yielded to the pressure on him and informed me that he was bringing charges against me — I think he thought of it as a court martial — under the AAUP 1940 *Statement of Principles on Academic Freedom and Tenure*, on the ground that in the letters to my representatives I did not "make every effort to indicate that [I] was not

135

an institutional spokesman." The Board of Supervisors had spoken for the institution in a manifesto declaring that Negroes were unwanted and unwelcome as students at LSU. In the heat of the hubbub, printed signs appeared overnight on every rest room and drinking fountain on the campus: "For White Only." Just as quickly, some witty students put signs on all the trash receptacles: "For White Trash Only."

To escape from the miasmic exhalations that were polluting LSU, I resigned in December, 1960, my resignation to be effective at the end of the school year. My wife resigned as Head of the Humanities Division of the LSU Library. Her friends, although supportive, then became afraid to talk to her except when well hidden in the stacks. The President of the LSU chapter of the AAUP was a stool pigeon for the General and a direct pipeline to his office. My friends were dwindling but brave: "Stay in there and fight. We're behind you." They were so far behind me that they were never going to get in the line of fire. A stream of letters and testimonials from my loyal graduate students, delivered by hand to the General's office, went unanswered and unacknowledged. My undergraduates were paralyzed with fear. The most intelligent of them, on whom I had counted as a witness if I had to stand trial, wept as he told me that his father was an employee of the State Department of Transportation.

My resignation was "the only self-respecting thing I could do," according to the *London Economist*. It was reported in the state press that I had been forced to resign, a mistake which General Middleton corrected. No pressure was on me to resign, until the pressure on General Middleton made me want to resign. The reactionary Shreveport *Times* editorialized that the General had the right to fire me if he didn't like the way I parted my hair. So much for academic freedom.

I was still under investigation by the legislature's Joint Committee on Un-American Activities, or "Un-Louisiana Activities," as some put it. This committee made no effort to get in touch with me; evidently, I was being investigated in absentia. My home telephone was bugged, as was the Baton Rouge office of the ACLU. Happily, no crosses were burned in my front yard. My son, who was then a junior at University High School, had the pleasure of knocking the son of Governor Jimmy ("You are My Sunshine") Davis down a flight of stairs at school. The report of the legislative committee which appeared several months later, a forty-page document entitled "The Case of Dr. Waldo F. McNeir," was an exercise in vacuity containing nothing about me that wasn't already known. The most asinine part of it, intended to throw suspicion on my wife for her "Un-American" activities, revealed that her Humanities Division did not have a single publication of the John Birch Society among its holdings.

As soon as my resignation was known in the profession, I received some offers from universities that harbored "nigger lovers." I had unwittingly become a *cause célèbre*. Some universities implied that they were interested in me as a martyr to academic freedom, a refugee from a new wave of Simon Legreeism in the South. I had to steer clear of these sentimental notions. The real "martyrs" to academic freedom in the South during the throes of racial segregation were those teachers whose family ties held them, or whose age made a new career elsewhere unfeasible.

An offer from the University of Oregon seemed attractive. It was soon widespread that I was going to Oregon at a salary twice what I had received at LSU, an exaggeration. The Shreveport *Times* fulminated that it hoped the good people of Oregon knew what they were doing. Unquestionably, Oregon enjoyed a more salubrious moral climate than Louisiana at all levels of government. Oregon had sent Wayne Morse to the Senate. The Pacific Northwest was a beautiful region. As for the state university, its faculty had a record of vigorously upholding academic freedom. Arthur Flemming, after serving as Eisenhower's Secretary of HEW, had just accepted the presidency. The English department, under the leadership of Kester Svendsen, a respected Miltonist and a classmate of mine at North Carolina, had attracted a strong faculty that was getting stronger. My family and I went there, happy that Oregon had chosen us and that we had chosen it.

Students at Oregon seemed easy going in speech, dress, and manner. They were unhaunted by shadows of the past. The girls, many of whom wore overalls and were a little broad in the beam,

137

were not overtly stalking a husband like the Barbie dolls and the anachronistic plantation belles down in Dixie. The men, many of them unkempt, were outdoor types without trying to project a macho image. In general, they responded to Shakespeare in my sophomore classes. I was surprised and pleased when I saw no shuffling of papers, looking at their watches, picking up the *Daily Emerald* to rustle and read, or premature breaks for the door. Ye gods, I thought, they're interested in Shakespeare, interested in what I'm saying. Even the C students were interested. I began to overcome my elitist attitude toward honest mediocrity.

One spring term I found a better way than the lecture-and-discussion method of presenting Shakespeare to sophomores in our three-term sequence. The idea came from a political science major in one of my classes, during a Convocation called so that students and faculty could evaluate their respective roles in the educational process, and discover ways of improving them. My student thought there was too much lecturing and too much un-profitable discussion in class; he advocated as much audio-visual presentation as literary interpretation to help to bring alive the plays that were studied. "Let's do it," I said. The University had an excellent audio-visual department, with much audio-visual material on Shakespeare. Better still, the Oregon Shakespearean Festival, the oldest in America and one of the state's chief cultural assets, was within easy reach in Ashland, where capacity audiences saw stunning productions of the plays on the outdoor Elizabethan stage all summer, and in the spring they could see the plays in indoor productions in the new and superbly designed Angus Bowmer Theater.

This was the beginning of a new and popular course, The Ashland Plays, offered in spring and summer terms. When I taught this in collaboration with one of my doctoral candidates, and later with the aid of several good special assistants, we used some novel ploys: the class (usually about sixty students) was divided into small groups for discussion of suggested topics; each group chose its own recorder and leader; the conclusions of the group were presented to the class by the group leader. Some lively exchanges brightened these proceedings, while I intervened only as arbiter of an impasse. During the term, volunteer groups worked on special projects such as a performance of Elizabethan music, the staging and direction of a scene or the acting of a scene, the construction of an Elizabethan theater, a stage design for one of the plays, or any bright idea of their own. The class had to attend at least one of the Shakespeare plays in Ashland, and write a review of it. The grand finale was always an Elizabethan banquet prepared from Elizabethan recipes by volunteer cooks. These were gala occasions, to which everybody came in fetching "Elizabethan" costume.

During my sojourn at Oregon I had a heyday with the Renaissance. I taught a three-term course in Shakespeare (comedies, histories, tragedies), and a one-term course in Spenser, besides seminars from time to time on *King Lear*, Shakespeare's problem plays or his romances, Marlowe, Sidney, Spenser, and Jonson, as well as courses on the Continental backgrounds of the English Renaissance, and Elizabethan prose and poetry. I taught two courses, or six hours a week, always including one section of the sophomore Shakespeare sequence. Every year I was able to direct one or more Ph.D. dissertations, and I was proud of the fact that my Ph.D.s got good positions at respectable institutions, that is, before the present dearth of jobs in the humanities.

In the stormy period when student tempers were exacerbated by the shameful war in Vietnam, Oregon had its rather belated violent demonstration. It occurred in April of 1970, when a motion to abolish ROTC was defeated by a faculty vote of 199-185. The students were especially angered by the narrow margin of defeat. A crowd of 300 or 400 people sacked the ROTC building, police were summoned, rocks were thrown, the police used tear gas and arrested seven persons. Some of my erstwhile colleagues down in Louisiana may have been surprised that I was not involved. In fact, I voted against the motion to abolish ROTC on the ground that it was intended to suppress an organization that was detested at the time; but banning it would have been a clear violation of the First Amendment. The nation-wide disturbances subsided as the social outcries of students in the 1960s were replaced by their apathetic shrugs in the 1970s. At the University of Muenster in 1968, a year in which bloody riots rocked many European universities, I teased my German students in placid North Rhine-Westphalia because they hadn't put on a single demonstration for me, hadn't made a single outcry.

I think I became a better teacher in the last decade or so of my unexciting career; I might give myself a B. I said I had become more tolerant of honest mediocrity. I never aimed to be a spellbinder, a crowd pleaser, a thunderer, a raconteur, or a charmer, although I have known some good teachers who employed these styles. I had a tendency to lose myself at times, not really thinking about what impression I was making on the students. They may have thought I had lost contact with reality, like Swift's philosophers on the flying island of Laputa. It felt very natural to be up there at the lectern or standing behind a table, just being myself and talking about things relevant to the literary work under analysis that I felt were important and that I was interested in, and trying to get the students interested in them, too.

I never thought that teaching and research were in conflict, and I can't draw a very clear line between preparing for a class and doing scholarship. With undergraduates, of course, I knew I couldn't assume they would know that *The Merchant of Venice* isn't anti-Semitic; but the notes I jotted down when getting ready for such a class were not scholarly. With a sophisticated graduate class or seminar, my teaching and my research complemented each other, or validated one another. Let me illustrate. One time when I was teaching *Henry IV, Part 1*, it struck me that the second tavern scene in the play (II,iv) has not only the hilarious role-playing of Prince Hal and Falstaff, but also has the structure of a miniature five-act drama. We discussed this possibility in class. The students tested the theory further in some papers that they wrote and on their final take-home exams, and found that the same kind of scene structure is fairly common in other plays of Shakespeare. So I wrote an article on the scene in *Henry IV, Part 1*, where I had first noticed it. On other occasions, at least for me, teaching and research worked well together.

Since my retirement as Professor Emeritus, and my wife's retirement as Associate Professor and Documents Librarian Emeritus, we have lived in Houston, where we first met as students at Rice. Thomas Wolfe was wrong; you can go home again. We're glad to find that integration is visibly operative here. I continue to write, publish scholarly stuff, and hold onto my academic connections. We continue to travel and thus avoid provincialism with extended trips to Europe, to the Far East, or back to Eugene to visit friends and to be with our son and our three grandchildren. We go to professional meetings and conventions wherever and whenever our kind of enjoyment, social or intellectual, promises new experiences.

William James Fulbright, born in Sumner, Missouri, April 9, 1905, was educated at the University of Arkansas and, as Rhodes scholar, at Oxford. His law degree was awarded at George Washington University. The Honorable Mr. Fulbright, distinguished senator from Arkansas for thirty years, is renowned in academia as law professor and president of the University of Arkansas. Believing that United States foreign policy was bound "to old myths" and blind "to new realities," Senator Fulbright established a program of student exchanges with other nations and scholarships for graduate study, research, teaching and professional training overseas.

William Fulbright

The Politics
of Survival

When we reflect that for thousands of years the human race has employed its many talents and a great part of its resources in a never-ending struggle for power and advantage over fellow human beings, are we reasonable to expect these habits of centuries to be changed or abandoned in the years since 1945? It would be most unusual if suddenly people began to be sympathetic and understanding of people of a different culture toward whom they have long been hostile. We shall not suddenly become new men.

Now, in addition, the dikes of human civilization are pressed by exotic new dangers — the rapid exhaustion of the world's fossil fuels, the persistent shortage of food, the growth of population at rates exceeding the earth's capacity to sustain new life, the pollution and even destruction of much of the human environment. Diverse as they are, these happenings have one common characteristic: in the long run, they profit no one and endanger everyone. Together they have radically altered the circumstances of human life upon the earth. And as our circumstances have changed, so must we change the way we conduct our affairs — from an obsolete politics of rivalry and advantage to a new, cooperative politics of survival.

143

Confronting Crisis

Can we do it? I feel just about certain that we can — but much less certain that we will. As always, the imponderable is human nature — whether it will permit us to do what we can do, and by and large, know we ought to do. The capacity to reason and analyze problems objectively is of course one trait of human nature, but not, I fear, its most conspicuous one. Arrayed against the power of reason are our traditional beliefs, prejudices and rivalries, of which the most formidable are usually associated with religion, education, nationalism or ideology. Their frequent effect — as applied to making war, for example — or to population growth — is to disarm our rational intelligence and to prevent us from doing what we ought to do.

In view of man's long and dismal history of violence generally — and of aggression especially — toward people of different cultures, is there any reasonable basis for hope that we may create a more peaceful and cooperative relationship among the nations of the world?

Granted that it is more difficult for man to alter his traditional beliefs and prejudices than it is for the dog to walk on two legs, nevertheless man is endowed with the capacity to reason, even though it has not yet been highly developed. Is there anything that we can do now to develop this capacity to reason and to bring about a change in the attitude of people toward the people of other countries?

Adlai Stevenson, a great citizen of America and the world, used to remind us that there is nothing in the human environment to prevent us from bringing about fundamental changes in the way nations conduct their relations with each other. The obstacles are within us, in the workings of the human mind. The problem is one of fundamental attitudes.

What is required, in the words of the British poet Stephen Spender, is "some kind of mutation of human consciousness." "What stares us in the face," he writes, "is that unless the practical becomes practicable, the experiment which is human life on this planet will probably fail."

Mr. Spender has, as great poets often do in a few words, indicated the nature of our problem: the need for "some kind of mutation of human consciousness."

Forty-four years ago, at the request of the League of Na-

144

tions, Albert Einstein and Sigmund Freud, two of the world's most powerful intellects, considered the question: "Is there any way of delivering mankind from the menace of war?"

In Freud's view, there was "no likelihood of our being able to suppress humanity's aggressive tendencies," but he also noted that in the course of evolution, mankind has attained a measure of cultural development and a strengthening of the intellect which gave us at least a limited capacity to control our primitive instincts and our inclination to use force rather than reason. Without predicting when or even whether humanity would put an end to war, Freud placed his hope in two factors: "man's cultural disposition, and a well-founded dread of the form that future wars will take."

Since that exchange of views in 1932, the horrible destruction of advanced technological warfare has enhanced enormously the dread of war, with the result that that factor, for the time being at least, continues to be the most effective restraint upon the resort to violence by the major nuclear powers. The enormous stockpile of nuclear weapons already in existence may sustain the "balance of terror" for a time — perhaps for a long time — but it seems inconceivable to me that peace can survive indefinitely on the basis of fear alone. Therefore it behooves us to turn to Freud's first factor: man's cultural disposition.

"All that produces ties of sentiment between man and man must serve us as war's antidote," Freud wrote to Einstein. Until those ties are developed among nations, the peace of the world will remain in chronic jeopardy.

In seeking the antidote for war, we are caught in a dilemma — can we devise means of disciplining the primitive impulse to use force in international relations which are both bold enough to eliminate or reduce the danger of nuclear war and modest enough to be within the limits of feasibility imposed by the present state of human cultural evolution?

There is no ready answer to this dilemma, but there is hope, and that hope consists primarily in the promise of transnational education for accelerating the cultural evolution of the human race. Living and learning with the people of different cultures from our own — in their schools, their cities, and their homes — is the most effective way to expand the boundaries of human wisdom, empathy and perception. We have had sufficient experience with international cultural exchanges to justify a major effort to expand these measures with a reasonable expectation that the participants in these exchanges will gradually become influential within their countries, and can turn their respective foreign policies toward a more cooperative attitude and away from the traditional ruthless and often violent competition for power and advantage.

I am sure that many of my readers have had, as I have had, the experience of living among — and with — the people of different social and political traditions and customs. Is it not true that you have found that many of the individuals with cultural characteristics quite different from your own are, nevertheless, far from being offensive or unattractive?

Is it not also true that, as you have acquired an understanding of the history and the reasons for these differences, you have found it possible to communicate and to reason with the foreigners — and have amicable relations with them — and that in a large measure the differences have appeared less sharp and less significant than they formerly seemed to be?

And beyond all of that, is it not true that however much you disapprove of their different cultural characteristics, you recognize the futility and inhumanity of seeking to change their political and social structure and values by force and violence?

If the effects of living and studying abroad with people other than your own are as I have suggested, it indicates that the social and political attitudes, inbred and traditional as they are, nevertheless may yield to our common humanity and to our desire to survive, and enable us to reconcile these differences by rational and peaceful means.

In the course of the last thirty years, I have met hundreds of young men and women — and professors — who have worked and studied in foreign lands. With few exceptions, they were favorably disposed toward their erstwhile hosts. There has been a "mutation in their consciousness" with regard to people of a different culture. I submit that when we have many thousands, instead of hundreds, of such people in positions of influence in the councils of the governments of the members of the United Nations, the "sentiments which bind man to man" (to use Freud's words) may be strong enough to restrain the mindless and arrogant drive for power which has afflicted mankind for so many centuries.

In addition to a major expansion of cultural exchanges, I wish to propose that there be initiated and sponsored a festival of the performing arts. The performing arts require people to use their unique human qualities, their intellect, their compassion, their capacity for empathy and their appreciation of beauty. In the creation of dramatic, or literary, and especially musical performances, people become aware of their essentially human attributes as distinguished from their physical prowess which they have in common with other creatures.

Physically, men are in many respects inferior to other animals who can run faster and farther and jump higher, but no other animal can compose a symphony or an opera — or play the piano or violin like Rubinstein or Menuhin.

The performing arts respond to man's yearning for beauty and for harmonious relations with other people. They elicit a peace of mind and calm the restless spirit. The performing arts encourage the kindly and benevolent qualities within us and suppress our selfish and malevolent passions.

The arts, especially music, have the power to reach across all barriers of class, caste, color, and language, and touch the hearts of all kinds of people. The arts can help bring about that mutation of consciousness and the development of those sentiments which bind men to men.

Walter Lippmann, in his moving tribute to Pope John XXIII, in 1963, wrote that "the universal response which Pope John evoked is witness to the truth that there is in the human person, however prone to evil, an aptitude for goodness. That is why we must never despair that the world can be better than the world we live in."

And so it is with all of us. We do not despair of the future of our world. We still believe, as Woodrow Wilson believed, that the common interests of mankind may be served by peaceful means.

Alice R. Bensen, born February 14, 1911, in Charlotte, Michigan, attended Washington University, St. Louis, the Sorbonne, University of Paris, and achieved the Ph.D. degree at the University of Chicago. She has taught at Valparaiso University, Indiana, and at Eastern Michigan University, Ypsilanti. Professor Bensen holds the Phi Beta Kappa key and has turned her enthusiasm from professoring to writing — and international travel. "In retirement," she says, "one does miss one's classroom — or perhaps one takes it around with him as the hermit crab his borrowed shell!"

Alice R. Bensen

Cats in Air-Pumps

"*Kennst du das Land?*" Mignon asks her lover, and, voicing her nostalgia for Italy — "*dahin! dahin!*" — she describes her homeland to him so that he can share it too. (And so that we can share it too. And on and on.)

Lucky are those whose parents begin opening out these further worlds to them early in life. We may lead our students to be such parents. My mother used to recite passages from Shakespeare to me while I "helped" her with the housework. She delighted in sharing with me many other exciting passages of verse and prose: "Hound of the Temple — stain to thine Order — set free the damsel! Traitor of Bois-Guilbert, it is Ivanhoe commands thee! — Villain, I will have thy heart's blood!" or "Day unto day uttereth speech, and night unto night showeth knowledge. There is no speech nor language where their voice is not heard."

A less lucky friend, now in her fifties, having just failed to see the point of a joke, confessed that in her schooldays she had never been able to see any meanings that were not set forth explicitly. (What "voice" have the sun, stars, and moon?) Perhaps no parent or teacher had made the process of imagining very exciting. Or perhaps she had had instilled in her the too prevalent

149

distrust of anything not strictly factual. My grandmother told how, as a child, she had proudly made up a story that began with a cow having a dream; her mother, in disgust, interrupted: "Cows don't dream!" (But here the imaginative turns out to have been the more factual . . . .)

Faced on occasion with a classroom of students who seem locked in the rigor of negative attitudes, the instructor may well long for a flock of Milton's hungry sheep. But the second, accusatory, half of the line needs sufficient attention. Some instructors, on the defensive, fear to "give themselves away" — to be suckers or patsies — if they let the students see the value that they find in certain work or passages. (But do actors on the stage shield themselves from this risk?) To be sure, some sensitive instructors may feel that they must protect the work itself from sneers by covering up its vulnerable finenesses by a matter-of-fact or even hard-boiled treatment: "This is a boy-meets-girl . . ."; "What he's saying is . . . ." Like the frustrated youth in Joyce's "Araby," they do indeed manage to bear their chalice safely through a throng of foes. But the foes, if indeed they are foes, remain thirsting. Some instructors feel that the current Zeitgeist requires them to choose this fallacious process of "reduction." Faced with a seemingly negative audience they join in the prevalent negativism: "This is *only* another 'boy-meets-girl . . .'; 'he's *only* saying . . .'; 'this old bromide . . . .' " The wittier ones may indeed carry on this procedure with some coruscation, and of course a sturdy work of art can retain its integrity against fun and Moorish darts; but by overusing this technique these instructors with sneering teach the rest to sneer. Reduction is not exposition. How much more appropriate than this safe negativism is the acceptance of the risk of giving the invitation "Come!" — inducing everyone to join in a sailor's "Come-all-ye . . . !"

The instructor setting forth on his or her presentation with courage and excellent intentions may find puzzling guideposts: "The letter killeth, but the spirit giveth life" and the twentieth-century critic's rebuttal "The spirit killeth, but the letter giveth life." Most of the difficulty vanishes if the opening clauses are recognized as overstatements; the second clauses carry the heart of the message: surely both the spirit and the letter are requisite to the total life of the work. A music teacher used to direct me to practice, in alternation, playing a piece through "up to speed" (or somewhat so!) without regard to the multitudes of wrong notes and then slowly and cautiously playing all the notes right — the full meaning of the piece required the integration of both elements. One may, in the current rat-race, omit the meaning of nonce-words in the less important passages, but Hamlet's "By heaven, I'll make a ghost of him that lets me!" is pretty pointless is one doesn't take time to recall "let and hindrance" or a "let ball."

Because the unabridged dictionary is usually not at hand at his place of study, the student may not receive much-needed aid from the Webster Companion. (And even if he owns a desk dictionary, he may never have learned to use it adequately.) This is a major challenge to the instructor. Eventually the student must be brought to see the advantage of knowing that "tele-" means not tell but "at a distance" (the new, wondrous element in the invention of the "tele-" instruments); that "geo-" words concern the earth, "iatr-" doctors. The letter that giveth life can even be the letter of the alphabet, as in the interesting variants "match, make, mate"; in the history revealed in "cantor, chantey, chant," and in our un-English pronunciation of the *ch* in Michigan and Chicago.

A student who reads *Intruder in the Dust* only in an overall way may miss such elements as the revealing sequence of breakfasts — at the home of Lucas Beauchamp, of Chick's mother, and of the Gowries. He may need help in seeing that Lucas' row of cans, bottles, and shards set into the ground in front of his cabin indicates proud neatness, not sordidness; the "letter" of the row of cans and the "spirit" implied by what we have seen of Lucas' conduct combine here to give the true meaning.

Attention to technicalities will offer the type of student who is usually puzzled by "interpretation" something he can grasp. Gilbert and Sullivan's Lord Chancellor laments that he must give away in marriage his pretty young wards — "And one for him and one for he" — and then extrapolates: "and one for you and one for ye, and one for thou and one for thee — but never no never a one for me!" Ogden Nash offers such passages as, ". . .

what would you do if you were up a dark alley and there was Caesar Borgia/And he was coming torgia?"

Pope, Johnson, Goldsmith & Co. ask us to be on the alert as their decasyllabic lines divide 6/4, 4/6, 2/8, 5/5, etc. Chaucer challenges us to guess what seint he is going to evoke in line 2 to cap the end-word in line 1. How is Dylan Thomas, in the next tercet, going to use his repeating-line "Do not go gentle into that good night"?

Many students read metric verse as if it were merely prose because no one has pointed out to them (and it isn't, perhaps, easy to do) how the underlying meter is one thing and the sentence rhythms set to this metrical scheme are another — with the resultant exciting tensions of counterpointing. To many students this is a revelation (and to some instructors).

Returning to "das Land," but at the geographical level, a friend in Earth Sciences requires each student in his courses to read at least one literary interpretation of the area under study. Nowadays, when almost everyone travels about, how much is added to a trip to California if one knows Norris' *The Octopus*, Gary Snyder's poems on the Sierra, Mark Twain's and Bret Harte's goldrush stories, and Jeffers' lyric and dramatic poems on the coast and mountains of Big Sur; to a trip to New Orleans if one has read *Old Creole Days* or Kate Chopin's stories; to the long drive across the great plains if one has felt the dangers and hardships of the settlers recreated in *My Antonia, Giants in the Earth*, or any one of dozens of novels and memoirs. Fodor and the phrasebook may turn out to be less important preparations for Europe than *Les Misérables* (in translation if necessary), *Bread and Wine, The Magic Mountain, Metamorphosis, Don Quixote* or *The House of Bernarda Alba, War and Peace*; when one comes, even in a car, to that still barren intersection where three ways meet, it is good to be able to recall the fated encounter between the young man, fleeing the oracle, and his unrecognized father.

Otherwise,

> Like cats in air-pumps, to subsist we strive
> On joys too thin to keep the soul alive.

Dwight Bolinger was born in Topeka, Kansas, August 18, 1907. Educated in Kansas (except for achieving the Ph.D. degree at the University of Wisconsin), he taught in Kansas, eventually, however, leaving the Midwest for the west coast and points between but finally arriving at Harvard, where he remained. He has been exchange professor in Costa Rica, Sterling fellow at Yale, Haskins Laboratories Fellow, a fellow at the Center for Advanced Studies in the Behavioral Sciences, and an American Academy Arts and Science fellow. His areas of interest are in English and Spanish linguistics.

Dwight L. Bolinger

Let's Change Our Base of Operations

Here is my indictment against the teaching of foreign languages: For all the lunar-orbiting technology that has given us machines to poke at language in undreamt-of ways, for all the committees that have confabulated under the auspices of the MLA, the NDEA, the NEA, and the AATs, for all the task forces that have turned our methods inside out and cognated new and better ways to present and drill the subjunctive, we still are ignorant of what our students' language-learning experience ought to be to make them want to undergo it and to come out wiser and more humane citizens as a result of it. We are the parents of 1932 who believed that the best method of rearing children was on a scientific regimen rather than with love. We were the American military in Vietnam, faced with a dedicated foe who laid his body on the line, yet who ourselves go on searching for a potion that when blown on the enemy will make him hygienically disappear, with a glad cry if possible. We are the Americans of the twentieth century, for whom science and its engineering handmaidens bring health, happiness, and learning in effortless abundance. We are America's teachers of foreign languages, who when something goes wrong jump to the conclusion that the trouble must be with the methods machine, and start tinkering with it

155

again. We have forgotten our own God-given gifts for reaching our students as human beings, and above all we have forgotten their divine gift for being reached if they have within them, or we can implant, a desire to be reached. We have persuaded all the wrong people — administrators — to ground the foreign language curriculum, PTAs to demand FLES, Congress to vote us money — but we have not persuaded our own clients, and at this moment when our triumph seems to be greatest, with language study written into the law in more than one state and with more students of all ages trying to learn how to speak something besides English, we have the feeling that we are, or soon will be, on the skids, because our students do not believe in us. Our major support now seems to be the requirements for college entrance and graduation. Yet while our other foundations have been eroded, this one is in danger of being knocked from under us. Let me read you portions from a couple of letters written by undergraduates at my institution to their tutors:

> "The language requirement made my academic career at Harvard a . . . frustrating and disappointing one. It killed . . . [my] chance to graduate with honors. It pulled down my grades in other subjects . . . . I worked very hard at French but to no avail . . . . I became so frustrated sometimes that I could not get any constructive studying done."
> "The damn language requirement will be my nemesis. I took a year's leave primarily because of the strain the language requirement placed on my other courses . . . . For those of us who have trouble with languages, the requirement is more than an inconvenience — it is a catastrophe."

It is much the same everywhere. Whatever the local picture, there is no mistaking what André Paquette, former Executive Secretary of ACTFL, refers to as "the groundswell which is leading to massive assault on all foreign language requirements at the college and university level."

When we look at the specific objections raised by students, we are reminded of the misunderstanding that patients often have of their diseases. They sense an acute but dimly located discomfort, and lash out at symptoms far removed from their causes. Sociolinguist Leon Jacobovits' report of a survey conducted at the University of Illinois at Urbana by the Liberal Arts and Sciences Student Council, answered by 838 students, showed that 80 percent felt they had to work too hard, that 61 percent felt that foreign languages kept them from studying other subjects that they wanted, that 53 percent considered what they learned in foreign languages courses to be useless for meeting graduate school requirements, that 80 percent thought that foreign languages did not help in creating better study habits, and 40 percent felt that foreign language study had actually been detrimental to them. Asked for their preferences, they favored a grammar-reading course slightly over an audio-lingual course, by 53 percent to 47 percent. These rationalizations read like a caricature of the terms in which we have tried over the years to sell foreign languages as a subject that everyone should take. We used to speak of mental discipline; more recently we have spoken of the salvation that audio-lingualism offers, of the value for meeting graduate school requirements. It is no wonder that our arguments are thrown back at us as a misreading of symptoms if we medicine men of foreign language teaching are unable to read them ourselves. For not a word is said in the survey about any value for insight in the great coding systems of the human race, or for the warmth of human association that engages us when we communicate with another human being in a tongue other than our own.

How is it that these values could escape us? I can think of no logical reason except that we have regarded them as by-products instead of essential ingredients in the learning process. We have assumed — if we have given the matter any thought at all — that in learning a language one must incidentally learn about language. And we have claimed the dividend of cultural sensitivity without ever doing much about it, except including a bit of second-hand appreciation in the form of cultural readings and literary texts on the theory — again if we have bothered to think about it — that when a French novelist writes a book to entertain Frenchmen, somehow or other the awareness that we want our students to acquire will shine through. The great truth that culture is transmitted by interpersonal communication has escaped us, and the greater truth that only this desire to communicate can make any difference to students when we ask them to practice a drill on personal pronouns. We thought all through

157

the 1950s and the 1960s that we had finally succeeded in democratizing the learning of a foreign language. We had brought it within the reach of eight and nine year olds, and had begun to make everybody talk, not just read, which is what you do when you come face to face with another human being. Yet all we accomplished was to improve the means a little bit. The ends, as far as our classes were concerned, were essentially the same as before: they were the successful handling of canned communications. In place of some of the books, we now had tapes. In place of some of the pictures, we now had video. And in place of the excitement and challenge of getting a meaning across to someone of our age and interests, we had, well, we had the teacher. In short, by every conceivable artifice we had either the same old substitutes or more sophisticated substitutes for *them*, and our students went as unnourished as ever with the real thing.

If this seems to carry the touch of Jeremiah as well as of the mystic, let me explain why our misunderstanding of our role involved us so excruciatingly with student protest, making us the symbol of what students opposed instead of what we could be, the embodiment of what they championed. That generation of college students, and more and more that of high school students, were faced with accumulations of pointlessness that drove many of them literally mad. They faced through half of their young adulthood the threat of being sent to die in a war, the explanations of which one week contradicted those of the week before. They were trained in skills that were destined to serve ends that made no sense to them. And in place of ends, at a time of life when ends and goals must be chosen and exert a stronger pull than ever before or after, they were given formalisms. The cry for relevance in the schools was of a piece with the cry for relevance in the church. Scholastic requirements went the way of the Latinate confession. If religion and the schools can do nothing for men as men, but only fit them for a place in a frozen order of things, then both are degraded.

I mentioned that we could be the embodiment of what students champion. The definition of this lies in the growing literature on bilingualism, which, in Jakobovits' words, gives "evidence that becoming bilingual carries with it the tendency of becoming bicultural." One could almost paraphrase one of the

158

most admirable aims of today's intelligent youth by those two words, "becoming bicultural," aims embodied in Vista, the Peace Corps, and social action groups on every campus seeking people-to-people contact. This was the generation that popularized the term "manipulative" to apply to social controls that were exerted in favor of social structure rather than in the interest of those manipulated. For those who are familiar with Wallace Lambert and his associates, the near synonymy of "manipulative" and "instrumental" will be apparent: the instrumental learner of a foreign language studies it to fulfil some extraneous goal, like becoming a translator or interrogating a prisoner of war. The integrative learner studies it because he is drawn to the people who speak it and to their culture. We have honed our tools to a feather edge for instrumental learners, but done little for integrative ones. These fight us the way a thwarted child fights his parents, wanting them to do something for him, not knowing what it is, only that something is wrong. If we cannot find the wisdom to couple our subject with its natural motivations in a person-to-person situation, then we are lost even if Congress makes foreign language study a requirement by Constitutional amendment.

What I am going to propose may appear to have a political ring: "If you can't lick 'em, join 'em." Rather, I would like to think of it as a regrouping of alliances in tune with our times. It is absurd for psychologists, sociologists, and philosophers to sit on the opposite side of the table from us, glaring our way while we glare back. If we only realized it, we are their natural allies, and if we were playing our part as we should, they would be ashamed to oppose us. This part demands that we put aside the textual emphasis of our courses and put in its place a new kind of content, with both an intellectual and a practical side. The practical side demands that our students be brought into face-to-face communication, from the first week of their classes, with native speakers of the language they are learning. The intellectual side demands that as our students learn they be given some insight into what is happening to them, a grasp of the relativity of their coding system seen from the vantage point of a different scheme of structuring meaning. I don't pretend that the change will be easy. I foresee practical difficulties that to many will seem impossible and will lead them to invent excuses for not making any adjustment. Some will say that it is all the fault of the audiolingualists, that we should never have abandoned grammar-translation and should hie ourselves back as fast as possible. Others will say that the trouble is with our lock-step methods of teaching — that we should build storybook laboratories and install in them a regal abundance of step-increment programs, where students can put on their auto-instructional space suits complete with footswitch, headphones, microphone, videotape, and stereoscopic glasses, and commune by themselves with the infinite, each proceeding at his own pace. Still others will turn to some faddish application of transformational-generative grammar, having no more connection with the real thing than much that passes for a "linguistic method" had with the structuralism of the fifties. Let me try to describe the steps that I think should be taken. We will find, I think, that they do not affect our methods of teaching so much as they affect the setting in which it takes place and the perspective on it that the student gets, to give it meaning in terms of his interests.

First, there is the question of what language should be taught. Most of us who advocate the teaching of a foreign language will argue that it does not make much difference — that it is the experience of learning a foreign language that our schools should provide for. If that is true, then I would say that for the health of the community, for social evangelism, and for the motivation for learning that live contact can give, the choice should be the language that is spoken by the most accessible ethnic group. If we have a high school in a city where there is a Polish community, then the language should be Polish. If the school is in a rural area near a Navaho reservation, the language should be Navaho. If the children themselves come for the most part from families that still speak Yiddish or Basque or Japanese, then these should be the languages. The reasons are almost too obvious to need emphasis: raising the self-esteem of ethnic groups and their children in the schools, giving a purpose to our young people whose imaginations are fired by the ideal of service but whose efforts in their own community are too often frustrated by linguistic barriers, and creating a setting in which learning satisfies an immediate need.

Dwight L. Bolinger

A second question, related to the first one of what foreign language should be taught, is whether any foreign language needs to be taught at all. The proposal to use ethnic groups might fall on hard times if there were no ethnic groups around. I would be inclined then to favor teaching the language of any minority group, which means simply that we view other dialects of English as if they were foreign languages for the purpose of satisfying a language requirement, teaching white children in Washington, D.C., for example, the dialect of the black children in the same area, with its fascinating lexical and grammatical differences from other kinds of English. All the purposes I have mentioned will still be served: community health, social service, and motivation by direct communication. Learning another dialect of English can be just as revealing, of the same things (including the non-inferiority of *any* language or dialect), as studying a foreign language, and could be a wiser choice in many communities. But I will blunt my sword by denying any intention of having Boston children speak Brooklynese when they recite the catechism. That would be as out of place as having them recite it in Russian. A dialect, as well as a language, has its time, place, and audience.

A third question is what we should do about materials. How is one to teach Basque if there are no textbooks on Basque for English-speakers? The idea seems absurd. Yet it was not absurd for the teachers of Burmese in the Army Specialized Training Program during World War II who had to bring in informants and work up their own materials. And isn't there another sense in which we *must* create some of our own materials? No two cities, no two schools, and no two classes, even of beginning French, have identical students with identical needs. It is a lucky teacher who can find a prefabricated text that exactly fills the bill. Most of us have to do some improvising, and I am suggesting now that our local needs come first and we ought to do a lot more. I think it is worth taking the chance that our own materials, if we know our subject and tackle the job conscientiously and intelligently, will be better for our students, being tailor-made for them, than the average text that tries to be everything to everybody. On this one score, an entreaty: we should not let the availability of certain materials determine the

161

Confronting Crisis

nature of our course. No responsible doctor diagnoses a disease in terms of the medicine that he happens to have on his shelf.

The steps I have outlined thus far have been largely sidesteps. What are the ones to take in order to make live communication a reality? It is hard to generalize. Each school will need to take advantage of whatever resources are most abundant. Suppose you are in a community like New Bedford, Massachusetts. According to one recent estimate, more than eight hundred Portuguese-speaking children who know no English are enrolled in the New Bedford schools. At a guess, since the town's population is around a hundred thousand, this means that between five and ten percent of all the schoolchildren in the New Bedford system are native speakers of Portuguese. The New Bedford educators have had more imagination than most in securing a Federal grant that will help to make the children literate in Portuguese at the same time that they are learning English — a procedure that experience has shown is the best road to bilingual literacy and the only alternative to remaining semi-literate in English. But the program stops short of reaping a full harvest. In its present form, like so many other social projects, it offers charity to its beneficiaries but expects nothing in return except a smooth transition to the life of the community — it represents, to put the matter crudely, a way of avoiding trouble. Imagine the sense of pride that those children would have if the English-speaking children of New Bedford were studying Portuguese and they could help! I can think of no better reason, if the schools of that city are going to have a foreign language requirement, for the language to be Portuguese.

Not all communities have resources as rich as this, but the opportunities are greater than most of us realize who have never bothered to look around us and inquire what languages and what dialects are spoken in our neighborhoods. There are more than three million American children who do not speak English, and there are thousands more who still command some other language than English. Had we acted with one voice as a profession we might have gotten accurate figures for every town and village in the United States, at least on who are the speakers of foreign languages. But the former Senator Ralph Yarborough's effort to move the Bureau of the Census to include the necessary

162

questions failed for lack of support. When a senator comes to us for help we should match his vision. Yarborough saw us as the social force that we could one day become and invited us to involve ourselves with dialect as well as with so-called foreign language. The vision is bilingual education.

The resources are there, surely for most of us, and at this point it is more crucial to decide whether we have the will to use them than to decide precisely how. It would be foolish to say yes blindly. We should know what we are taking up and what we are laying down. There is our traditional snootiness about language. We can no longer afford it. We shall have to learn to repeat with our Negro fellow-citizens, "Black is beautiful." Those of us who have had young native speakers of our target language in our classes, think back: have we ever made them feel inferior? Have we ever said, or thought, "He doesn't speak pure Spanish; he speaks Mexican"? Excuse my saying it, but this is the silk-gloved linguistic counterpart of the sign in a Texas restaurant that read, "No dogs or Mexicans served here." It may be true that an insignificant portion of the phonology, lexicon, and syntax of the Mexican child is regarded as substandard by other speakers of Spanish, but most of what he knows is teachable and the best way to help him hold onto it and improve it is for you and your other students to treat it with respect, of which the sincerest is imitation.

Finally, there are the goals we serve, the methods we use, and the evaluations we make. The goals must be found within language itself and in what it can do here and now to enable human beings to interact. The methods require no revolution; rather they should be added to, with individual students trying out their skills with native speakers from the beginning. And the grades we give should reflect more than the four skills plus the recollection of trivial facts: we need a measure of cultural awareness and of intellectual appreciation of language in its essence.

If we can make these adjustments, putting aside our prejudices and overcoming our fears, we may begin to do what we are uniquely able to do: give our children that empathy with others which they dimly realize is a condition of their survival, and the lack of which in part explains their restiveness with us.

Confronting Crisis

Perhaps Senator Yarborough was flattering us when he addressed himself to bilingual education as a social force: "It strikes me that all of us are in the business of improving one thing or another. My improving is done through legislation; yours is done through scholarship and teaching. And I think that through your efforts to understand and improve knowledge of and ability to use languages — communication — you are performing the most fundamental and important task of civilizing man." If this was flattery I suggest that we take it as gospel and do our utmost to live up to it. What comes first is truth — accuracy in linguistic description, authenticity of cultural models, and our truth to ourselves, our dedication. Next is clarity; truth is vain if it is unintelligible. The channels of communication — ink on paper, recording tape, film, teaching machines — are aids, no more, and are not where the real need for improvement lies. The medium is not the message.

Cleanth Brooks is a Kentuckian, born October 16, 1906, in Murray. His association with the southern writers at Vanderbilt is well-known, a chapter in the history of literary criticism. A Rhodes scholar, Brooks achieved B.A. and B.Litt. degrees at Oxford. He has since been honored many times by American universities. Brooks' teaching career at Louisiana State University from 1932-1947 was marked by his association with the *Southern Review*. He served as a fellow of the Library of Congress between 1951 and 1962, and was twice a Guggenheim fellow.

Cleanth Brooks

Forty Years of *"Understanding Poetry"*

My title is probably misleading. . . . The phrase "forty years" has, of course, a Biblical ring. One thinks of Noah's flood in which it rained for forty days and forty nights; and of Moses abiding on Mount Sinai for forty days and forty nights; and the Israelites wandering for forty years in the wilderness before they were allowed to enter the promised land; and Christ's fasting in the wilderness for forty days; and so on. A friend of mine who teaches Old Testament in the General Theological Seminary has told me that, for the ancient Hebrews, "forty" meant not a specific numerical period but simply "a long, long time." That's good enough for me. The forty years since 1938 — actually, now, some forty and a half — certainly seem to me a long time, and for those people who see the advent of *Understanding Poetry* as the coming of a blight, it must seem truly a long time.

Now for some of that ancient history. Robert Penn Warren and I found ourselves in the mid-1930s teaching at the Louisiana State University. We had overlapped a year at Vanderbilt in the 1920s and later we had overlapped a year at Oxford. Now in 1934 we had come together again. Among other things, each of us was teaching a section of the department's course in literary forms and types. Granted that Warren and I were young men ex-

167

Confronting Crisis

cited by the new trends in literature — Warren was already a published poet — and granted that our heads were full of literary theory — drawn from the poetry and critical essays of T. S. Eliot and from the then sensational books on theory and practical criticism written by I. A. Richards — nevertheless, our dominant motive was not to implant newfangled ideas in the innocent Louisiana sophomores we faced three times a week. Our motive was to try to solve a serious practical problem.

Our students, many of them bright enough and certainly amiable and charming enough, had no notion of how to read a literary text. Many of them approached a Shakespeare sonnet or Keats's "Ode to a Nightingale" or Pope's *Rape of the Lock* much as they would approach an ad in a Sears-Roebuck catalogue or an editorial in their local newspaper. For example, one of Warren's students, to whom he was teaching *King Lear*, would mournfully shake her head and mutter: "I just don't like to read about bad people."

Our students were not stupid. They were simply, if I may use a theological term, almost "invincibly ignorant." Nobody had ever tried to take them *inside* a poem or a story, or tried to explain how a poem *worked*, or, if I may borrow a phrase from Emily Dickinson, no one had shown them how a poem, in telling the truth, has to tell it *slant*. For all our students' previous reading and instruction had stressed one virtue only. The purpose of all discourse was to convey information and to deliver it straight. All must be rendered as plain as a pikestaff. Alas, the prose that our students themselves wrote was scarcely a model of lucidity and concision. In fact, the pressures toward direct statement had succeeded in killing their aptitude for poetry without teaching them how to write decent expository prose.

We found that the textbooks adopted at LSU for introducing students to literature were of almost no help at all. They were anthologies, devoid of notes, or if they did contain notes, the notes were confined to explanations of difficult words or to literary allusions or to biographical and historical facts. Thus, the text of Keats's "Ode to a Nightingale" would be headed with a short introduction that set forth the dates of Keats's birth and death, and described the occasion of his writing the poem, with perhaps a reference to the garden of the house in Hampstead where he was living and where, one evening, he had listened to a nightingale sing. The editor also usually added a bit of impressionistic criticism, such as praise for the ravishing beauty of the poet's evocation of an English garden in mid-May, or of his equally powerful evocation of the spell of a medieval romance through his reference to "magic casements, opening on the foam / Of perilous seas in faery lands forlorn." The typical textbook also added glosses on words like "Hippocrene" and "Darkling," and a note that the Ruth referred to was a woman whose story is told in the Old Testament.

Such factual notes were all to the good, but the lollipop of impressionistic criticism we could cheerfully forgo. For the student would not possibly understand what the editor's praise meant unless he could understand the poem — to which understanding the editor's rhetorical flourish contributed next to nothing at all. In short, the typical presentation of this great ode too often left the student-reader groping in another flowery darkness, a darkness much like that in which the speaker of the poem finds himself, moving through "verdurous glooms and winding mossy ways," unable to "see what flowers [were at his] feet." Someone protests: Yes, but a great poem doesn't *need* any teaching. Just read it; just attend to its cadences:

Darkling I listen; and, for many a time
I have been half in love with easeful Death.

Maybe so. But the average college freshman, when he simply listens to the poem, finds his situation "darkling" in another sense. Moreover, since at the age of 18 he is not even half in love with Death, no matter how carefully he listens the nightingale just doesn't speak to him; nor does the poem. . . .

What to do, then, confronted with problems like these and supplied with inadequate textbooks for coping with them? Warren, rarely ever at a loss and always bursting with energy, began composing a booklet to distribute to his section of the course. It was mostly on metrics, but he provided some remarks on imagery. He showed the booklet to me and invited comments, and I believe that it was I who suggested a few changes and additions to the pages on imagery.

The little booklet of some thirty pages was then mimeographed and we distributed copies to our students. A little later, we decided to do a full-dress book that would provide a text for teaching poetry, fiction, drama, and essays. The book was written, and brought out by the LSU Press in 1936. It was entitled *An Approach to Literature*. I must add that it was not received by the English Department with deafening cheers. It clearly cut across the grain of our colleagues' tastes and past training. Some of our comments on particular stories and poems aroused downright outrage. As I now realize, we must have appeared to be two very brash and bumptious young men who, from our Oxford experience, had got well above our raising. I quickly learned that *An Approach to Literature* was sometimes referred to in the department as *The Reproach to Literature*, a witticism that Warren and I began to use ourselves when one of us mentioned the book to the other. . . .

It was some time before we had any intimation as to whether we were having any success. The first really encouraging hint came in 1939 when the CEA, in conjunction with the MLA, held its annual meeting that year in New Orleans. Warren did not attend, but I did, and found myself at the banquet sitting next to William Clyde Devane, then Dean of Yale College. I was completely surprised when he told me that *Understanding Poetry* had been adopted at Yale for a remodeled freshman English course. The younger men in the department had staged, he told me, something like a mild palace revolution, got the character of the course radically changed — and *Understanding Poetry* adopted.

Understanding Poetry did begin to catch on. We proved to be accurate in our belief that we would encounter strong opposition, for we did. The opposition, as you would suppose, took a variety of forms. But the principal charge was that Warren and I meant to eliminate from the study of poetry all reference to history, biography, and cultural background. We had ignored these considerations. We evidently regarded them as completely unimportant, as if poems were not written by human beings. Just as young children were once told that they had been found under a cabbage leaf in the garden, Brooks and Warren had pretended that poems just appeared mysteriously in the pages of the *Oxford Book of English Verse* or some other such collection. Yet, since any poem was the expression of some human being, mind, the

170

proper way to study it was to learn all one could about that person, the period in which he lived, what he thought and had read, and the climate of ideas that had helped shape his mind and spirit. All of this we had heretically rejected.

Now let me remind you of the circumstances that governed the production of our little book. The graduate school discipline which had molded the typical instructor of the 1930s stressed background, cultural climate, biography, and history. It was long on these items but very short on the study of the poem as a work of literary art. This was the general situation in my own graduate school experience and I take it to have been also in Warren's. So in *Understanding Poetry* we were simply applying the grease to the wheel that squeaked worst. We expected the *instructor* to supply biographical and historical data, for we took it for granted that he was at least equipped to do that. In our limited space, in a book of small compass, we would try to supply something else — something that evidently wasn't being supplied by the current textbooks and apparently wasn't a part of the repertoire of the average instructor.

Actually, even in the 1938 edition of *Understanding Poetry* we did not leave out all consideration of the poet and his background. The other day I got out a copy of our first edition to check, and the main historical references are present. But give a dog a bad name and it's hard for him to shake it. We were to labor — I should say, still labor — under the imputation of neglecting biography and history. . . .

Hazard Adams, in his useful manual of literary theory entitled *The Interests of Criticism*, provides, I think, a sound account of what happened during the decades from 1938 to 1958.

> When the New Critics appeared, the philologists and cultural historians, in their own positivism, assumed that the New Critics were merely the aesthetes [of the nineties] again. Besides, several of these critics were professed poets. Poets had not been thought to belong properly in English departments.
>
> That is perhaps unnecessarily sarcastic, but sarcasm is at least true to the tone of the debate that raged in academia during the forties. Woe to the young graduate student caught in the crossfire! The matter comes up for mention here because the intellectual aims of the New Critics during this time were so often misconceived. The New Critics were not, as many of

the cultural historians seemed to think, trying to separate literature from life. Their view was that philological and historical scholarship had made literature disappear by converting it into linguistic specimen or historical document. The critic should read literature as if it were an art. This meant literature had to be distinguished from other modes of statement conceptual in nature and subject to rational standards or proof. The New Critics held that poetry was a mode of language with its own unique cultural value; it returned man from the abstraction of intellect to a contemplation of the particulars and complexities of individual experience.

A new pedagogical method, first formally espoused in Cleanth Brooks and Robert Penn Warren's *Understanding Poetry*, won a victory in academia, though here and there bands of defenders held out even after the war had ended, sometimes out of ignorance of events. The teaching of literature was fundamentally changed by these events; it has not and will not return to its former state.

As for Adams's last statement, I have some reservations to make. I shall return to his prophecy later on in this paper. But as to what he says generally in this passage, I heartily subscribe.

The fact that in the early editions of *Understanding Poetry* we played down background material in favor of emphasis on the poem as a literary artifact means no more than that we were stressing *intrinsic* criticism rather than *extrinsic*. I make use here of the distinction that Austin Warren and René Wellek were to make in their important book, *Theory of Literature*, which appeared in 1949. Extrinsic criticism has its importance, but neglect of intrinsic criticism leaves us without a proper criticism of the work of art.

The theoretical distinctions that I make use of here are well stated in two now celebrated but still frequently misinterpreted essays entitled "The Intentional Fallacy" and "The Affective Fallacy" by William K. Wimsatt and Monroe Beardsley. Some scholars who ought to know better have understood Wimsatt and Beardsley to say that poets don't have intentions, or that if they do, the intentions can be disregarded. What is really said by Wimsatt and Beardsley is something very different: to wit, that it is the intention *as realized in the poem* that counts. Realized intentions are primary evidence, whereas what the poet wrote to a

Cleanth Brooks

friend that he had intended to do, or what someone had overheard the author say was his intention is what a trial lawyer calls "hearsay evidence." We must not rely on hearsay evidence when first-hand evidence is available, and first-hand evidence *is* always available in the poem itself. . . .

This doesn't mean that one isn't eager to learn what the poet says he was up to. What the poet says is always interesting and is usually extremely helpful. But ultimately it has to be tested against the work itself.

"The Affective Fallacy" does not say — as some scholars seem to think — that the reader shouldn't be affected by a poem or that the poem is a coldly intellectual process, a puzzle to be worked out. What the essay does argue is this: that to judge a poem by exclaiming "Great" or "Lovely" or "Wow" is a very vague and unsatisfactory kind of criticism. Besides, readers vary. Whereas one reader on finishing a certain Auden poem may say "Wow! How fine it is!" another reader will say "Wow! I might have had a Tennyson poem instead." Poetry produces emotional effects, but any responsible criticism has to be more discriminating and more specific than a shout of approval or a grunt of disgust — or with several pages of rhetoric that amount to little more than "Wow!". . .

We have obviously tried to meet some of the criticisms that have been offered from time to time. Thus, we have in the later editions added a section of poems that are entirely bare of discussions or questions because some instructors have complained that we had not left enough scope for them. . . .

In the later editions we have added many more poems of the 1960s and 1970s. We have altered, I trust for the better, the arrangement of the poems very considerably. Most of all, we have clarified our own style, reduced some of the verbosity, and cleared up vague concepts. We have also added many more notes on the meaning of words, on the background of poems, and the cultural context out of which they arose. . . .

So much for some of the changes in *Understanding Poetry* from 1938 to 1976. These few hints must suffice. But now, some forty years after the first edition, what has been accomplished? What was the impact of the book? The range of opinion has been

173

wide. At one extreme, *Understanding Poetry* has been credited with altering the entire teaching of literature. The other extreme is represented by a professor under whom I did graduate work and who later would introduce me to a colleague by saying: "This is the young man who has done most to ruin the study of literature." True, he smiled when he said it, but I think that he more than half believed it. In any case, there are many who do believe it wholeheartedly. . . .

Well, which view is correct? Obviously it is not for me to say. I can hardly be allowed to judge my own case. That judgment will have to be made by others or perhaps left to posterity. Yet there are a few pertinent remarks that I think I can be allowed to make. *Understanding Poetry* has indeed made some kind of impact. . . .

Since 1938, textbooks that provide an introduction to poetry and to literature have radically changed; and I think, on the whole, they have changed in the Brooks-Warren direction. To me, some of these new books seem to be dilutions and trashy imitations. But a number of others, truth compels me to say, seem to me quite excellent. And why should they not be? Warren and I could not patent a method or a process, even if we had wanted to. If we had not written *Understanding Poetry*, in time some other person surely would have had to do so.

There has been, however, in the last decades, a sharp reaction against the badly misnamed "New Criticism," and *Understanding Poetry* has been heavily involved in this counterattack. I think that the so-called New Criticism is usually misconceived and that it is damned for faults of which it is not guilty. . . .

A few years ago Robert Langbaum, of the University of Virginia, came at the matter from a rather different angle. In his *The Modern Spirit*, 1970, he said in effect that there was no point in squabbling further over the merits and demerits of the New Criticism. What was valuable in it had been absorbed by members of the profession generally. Further debate was meaningless for the reason that everyone now routinely followed its principles and employed its techniques.

This is a verdict that I would be more than happy to settle for. Neither Warren nor I had ever been eager to emulate the fanatical young hero of Longfellow's "Excelsior" who bore "through snow and ice/A banner with this strange device," a man obsessed with planting his flag on some yet higher peak. (Someone has parodied Longfellow's poem, the last stanza of which tells us that when the youth's frozen body was at last found. "They opened up his hand and found,/Excelsior.")

In writing *Understanding Poetry*, our ambitions were modest, even grubby. We simply wanted to do something that plain common sense — never mind imagination — indicated someone ought to do. If, a generation later, one could honestly pronounce "Mission Completed," then that would be quite sufficient for us.

Yet I can't really accept Langbaum's or Adams's way of settling the issue. To my eyes, the mission has not been accomplished. Let me indicate why I say this. When I read PMLA or the other learned journals, or even our university quarterlies, I find much too frequently articles that make elementary mistakes in criticism, essays that show inept reading and silly distortions of meaning. Literary criticism has often degenerated into symbol-hunting and morality-mongering. If members of the profession who achieve publication do as badly as this, then what of the students that they teach? If gold will rust, then what will iron do?

There is plenty of evidence to be gathered from those very college students. I am not thinking here of that pathetic group of semi-literates who can scarcely read at any level and are almost incapable of writing simple English prose. I have called them pathetic, for I think many of them have been more sinned against than sinning, victims of an incompetent educational system. But that is another story and one that I shall not go into here.

No, I am thinking of some very bright students, among them a number of graduate students that I have been teaching during the last few years. They have minds and imaginations. They learn rapidly and they are grateful to be taught. For they are aware that they do not yet read literature with the sensitivity and at the depth required of a cultivated person. If it seems incongruous that graduate students can profit from a book designed for college freshmen, in this case the last edition of *Understanding Poetry*, it is nevertheless true. My Yale colleague

175

Confronting Crisis

Louis Martz has corroborated this estimate from his teaching Yale seniors. Bright students who had been allowed to skip the freshman course because of their competence in English were still lacking in the kind of attention to literary texts that *Understanding Poetry* was planned to give. Their sophomore, junior, and senior courses in English had just not supplied it.

So I am forced to conclude that Professor Langbaum's generous citation claims too much for us. We have won some skirmishes, even a few major battles, but we have not been able to consolidate our position and we have made no really important territorial gains. We have not won the war. The war goes on.

This may seem a rather melancholy conclusion. Yet I console myself with the reflection that the great issues are never finally settled. The perpetually lost causes are finally the only causes worth seriously fighting for. It would be naive to believe that one could insure that each succeeding generation would ask the right questions about a poem and invariably try at least to give pertinent answers. Human nature itself denies any such illusory hope. I am a realist. The war for true literacy will probably have to go on for as long as civilization itself.

Joe David Thomas, child of the New Year of 1908, is a descendant of Tom Sawyer, though Carrollton, Missouri, not Hannibal, was his birthplace. Educated at the University of Chicago, he taught at Rice University, Houston, for forty years. His teaching areas were bibliography, Victorian literature, modern drama, and fiction. For the last ten years, he has delighted audiences with his impersonation of Mark Twain. One of the founders of the College English Association, he has lent his inimitable wit and organizational ability to coordinating affiliates.

Joe D. Thomas

Integrate or Perish

When I was young in heart and limber of lip, I once spoke for a short hour by the University of Houston clock to a district workshop of the Committee for Integration of English Teaching in High Schools and Colleges. A mimeographed copy of my spiel came, by deftly contrived means, into the office of the then President of the then Rice Institute, who thought well enough of it to suggest its publication in the house organ of our campus. Archeopedagogues can read it in the October 1957 issue of *The Rice Institute Pamphlet* under the alluring title of "The Land of Heart's Desire."

Before proceeding, I must deal with a cavil that some sharp-eyed (and sharper-tongued) reader is bound to raise: if the author of this present essay is retired, how could he have been young in 1957? Well, in the first place, the speech had been delivered two years before it was printed. Clandestine smuggling of documents into presidents' bonnets and surreptitious infesting of their ears with fleas take time. More importantly, I retired early (at sixty-nine) and am still only in my seventy-second year. Anyway, I was a slow bloomer and my heart remained young an unconscionably long time.

179

Confronting Crisis

Those who put themselves on record in print would be wise if, like many of the Romantics of the early nineteenth century and even more of the Decadents of the *fin de siècle*, they spared their blushes in later life by dying young. I would weep for the chagrin of aging members of the Southern group of writers in this present century, who must tremble with constant fear lest someone maliciously quote from their pronouncements of forty or fifty years ago on the Social Question — except that I have nightmares of my own about hearing bones (or boners) from "The Land of Heart's Desire" rattling in my closet. The lecture-essay was built around the following thesis, boldly pointed up on the printed page with italic type: "It is impossible for the high schools to prepare the total population for the university, because *the university has nothing to do with the total population.*" I do not have to be reminded that *nous avons changé tout cela!*

The statement was naive even when I uttered it aloud on October 22, 1955, as a prolegomenon to my short hour on the platform. In my defense I can only say that I had spent the preceding quarter century in artificial educational situations. From the University of Chicago, elitist if not entirely elite, I had come to the Rice Institute, where about fifteen hundred young men and women were offered a higher education of (by intention, at least) first-rate quality, without payment of tuition. Laboratory and incidental fees were trivial by today's standards, and those who found even a free private education beyond their means had available a considerable number of small scholarship awards. In consequence, we had our pick of the best-qualified high school graduates of Houston, and more widely of Texas and the "marchlands" of neighboring states. As Rice University has since done, we could have gone national and even international, except for a lingering recollection that the founder, William March Rice, had intended his institute to benefit the struggling boys and girls of Texas, which had served him well in the decades following his arrival as a young merchant from New England whose entire stock of merchandise lay shipwrecked at the bottom of the sea. (Yes, Virginia, he was saved; in fact he came by another route — by land and river.) Seemingly he had also thought of the projected Rice Institute as a sort of polytechnic high school, but if so, the first president, who had earned a

German doctorate at Leipsic, must have persuaded the original trustees that high school is the same as *Hochschule*, which of course signifies a German institution of university grade. For years the Rice campus did not have a gymnasium, much less a *Gymnasium*.

The early institute, if not exactly a land of heart's desire (particularly in the depression years, of which my own arrival in 1930 was harbinger), was a kind of academic Shangri-La. Consequently — although I did have the grace to dub the phrase "horrendous" — I was able to differentiate "college material" from the mass population of the secondary schools. For that elite "material" I described an ideal preparatory curriculum of English studies (primarily composition), foreign language (preferably Latin), mathematics (through trigonometry), general science (with emphasis on scientific method), and broad historical studies. Without boasting of any special sagacity, for indeed my proposed curriculum was conventional enough in the older parts of the country and in the better large high schools of the hinterland (it was pretty much what I myself had received in Kansas City during the 1920s), I must say that the combination of studies I described would still be about as desirable as could be devised for the kind of students I meant then by "college material." I fear, however, that it will not be reflected in many transcripts of the late 1970s or early 1980s.

In spite of vast changes in the educational and social environment, the intention implicit in the name Committee for Integration of English Teaching in High School and Colleges remains the heart of our problem in providing a meaningful continuum between school and college. *We must integrate our curricula, or we shall perish.* If I have slipped a subtle change of phrasing past you, I beg you to stop and reflect. It is no longer our secondary curriculum for the college-bound "college material" that must be integrated with the colleges and universities, but the multiple curricula. Beginning two or three generations back, "everyone" began to go to high school, although it must be added that until just a few years ago the drop-out rate before graduation was considerably more than fifty percent. Now, in the same sense, "everyone" goes to college. The attrition rate is still enormous, but the same forces that have

181

Confronting Crisis

operated to oppose dropping out of high school are now being felt within colleges and universities. The truth is that we Americans are living longer, and indeed are just now reversing a seemingly progressive trend and beginning a movement for later rather than earlier retirement. Barring basic upheaval, we have the time and resources for a greatly extended period of education. Very possibly, the junior and community colleges (under some new designation) will develop analogously to the junior high (now "middle") schools in bridging and accommodating an expanded normal period of school attendance. There is certainly no reason why they must be limited to two years, or why they should not grant "terminal degrees" (as, indeed, many do at present) to some classes of students. I suspect that "college" will come to be exclusively the code word for intermediate institutions of higher learning, and that the more grandiloquent "university" will accelerate an already marked progress in swallowing up all others. Perhaps university work will eventually begin after what is now the sophomore, junior, or even senior year of college.

If I had my present way, tuition-free public education would be available to everyone up to the age of at least twenty-five, and possibly thirty. It would become the way of life for almost the total population until their arrival at full maturity, or until individuals voluntarily dropped out of the process. Under those circumstances, any talk about "college material" would be irrelevant, not to say ludicrous. The keyword would become curricula, a plural implying diversity. There would be curricula for physicians, for lawyers, for merchants, for accountants, for secretaries, for homemakers, for restaurateurs and bakers, for military officers and for the ranks, for the naval and the merchant marine, for all classes of engineers and technicians, for carpenters, for postal clerks and carriers, for plumbers, for automobile and aircraft mechanics, for linguists and translators, for farmers and ranchers, for diplomats and (if possible) statesmen, for business and industrial executives, for historians and philosophers and theologians, for teachers of all types and degrees, for painters, for musicians, for writers of many orders from creative to reportorial — for professionals and artists and artisans and craftsmen and functionaries of every description.

Joe D. Thomas

All would go to college or to the university or to both in sequence, or at least have the liberty and encouragement to do so.
The fruits of their experience would be genuinely educational
and not merely vocational, but on the other hand they would not
come out of school with undeveloped capability of "doing
anything." The opportunity to get education and training would
not mean any more than it does at present — that everyone
would have the option of becoming a doctor or a research
physicist or a college professor or a director of either a bank or
an orchestra. Nothing in education is sure and easy, but among
the least uncertain procedures is the testing of aptitudes. An
enormous expansion of the profession of counseling would
become an obvious necessity. Parenthetically (but importantly),
I will add that an even more enormous expansion of instruction
in literacy should infuse all the curricula. I have tried to think of
exceptions, without success.

Attrition would inevitably continue to occur. Beyond a certain age, perhaps one earlier than at present (say, fifteen), no one
should be compelled to stay in school. A major function of
counselors would be to make clear to potential or threatened
drop-outs that since almost all productive work was being done
by "college people," their chance of finding other than menial or
criminal employment for the long remainder of their life would
be slight. No doubt, skillful new techniques would gradually be
developed for educating youth to the importance of becoming
well educated. No doubt, too, a certain snowball effect would
come into play: as more and more young people remained in
classrooms or in various apprentice programs of learning to their
middle or late twenties, the freedom of the streets would come to
look less and less attractive to their doubtfully motivated peers.
Educational opportunity, if by no means a universal solvent for
human problems, may be as near to one as we shall ever come.

I fear that my "integrated curricula" will be detected as but
old "tracking" writ large. I shy away from the latter word in the
hope that some of its odium can be avoided by substitution of a
more highly faluting name, for — sadly enough — our greatest
difficulty is sheer snobbery. Many a sound and sensible
pedagogical proposal of college-bound tracks and technical
tracks has foundered on parental insistence that all the young

hopefuls were "definitely college material." My idea is that all tracks — oops! I mean, all integrated curricula — would be college tracks. "Everyone goes to college" could become a sort of PR slogan.

The real problem, of course, is the detecting of workable combinations of aptitude-and-inclination-and-sticktoitiveness early enough to prevent perpetual shifting of great masses of students from one curriculum to another. I take some comfort in the wise saw and modern instance that if we can put a man on the moon, et cetera. Luckily, if we ever do institute a system of free education to the age of twenty-five or thirty, there should be enough time for almost every youth to discover a true bent. Moreover, a certain amount of flexibility and overlap of curricula is desirable as well as unavoidable. Properly guided freedom of maneuver must replace our present state of chaos, where "everyone" (The quotation marks concede numerous and glorious exceptions. I should like to make a bow to the "magnet school" concept, now in its comparative but promising infancy.) takes a hodgepodge of high school courses of no particular tendency and then winds up in college with no reliable foundations for a meaningful continuation in some clearly defined direction.

I rejoice if I have overstated my case, but I know that the stated problem — whether overstated or understated — confronts us formidably. If we do not integrate our curricula, we surely shall perish. Then the men on the moon will either mourn or mock.

Margaret M. Bryant, a South Carolinian, was born December 3, 1900. She achieved her Ph.D. degree at Columbia and undertook a series of teaching positions, at length coming to Brooklyn College, where she was professor of English, eventually chairperson of the department, and later a member of the graduate faculty at City University of New York. A linguist, dialectician, and folklorist, Professor Bryant has acquired international reputation as a lecturer and visiting professor. Her *Current American Usage* is a classic reference work.

Margaret M. Bryant

An Abecedarian: from Jocassee to Brooklyn

When I finished high school and went off to college with my diploma in hand, my aim in life was to become a high school teacher. The women whom I admired most had been my teachers and I had been fortunate to have had excellent ones. Each had a college degree, good training or a natural instinct for teaching, and a devotion to her work and students that seemed unlimited despite that the profession, especially in my state, South Carolina, was rewarded poorly. Teaching was at the bottom of the wage scale. And, teaching was the only profession open to women in those days. Those were the horse and buggy days.

We live now in a changing world, a scientific world, where research goes on from the depths of the sea to the stratosphere, where trips to Mars or the moon hardly arouse excitement any more, where we talk of establishing colonies in outer space, and the younger generation look forward to working and living there. In this contradictory world, narrowing and widening at one and the same time, in this world where communication is all-important, where something happening in Zaire, Uganda, Indonesia, Tahiti, or some other exotic place, is flashed around the globe instantaneously, changes occur so rapidly that individuals find themselves forced to relinquish old ideas, habits, and tradi-

187

tions to keep abreast of the times. The movement from one kind of society to another is always difficult. One can get some inkling of what is happening today if one considers the upheaval of European society that occurred in the transition from Middle Ages to Renaissance.

When I departed from college with an A.B. degree and a great desire to teach, I went first to a place in what is now called Appalachia for fifty dollars a month. I had been hired as principal of a small school in South Carolina for the coming academic year, but I had not planned anything for the summer. At that time one out of four persons in the state could not read or write. The governor, at the urging of the South Carolina Federation of Women's Clubs, appointed an Illiteracy Commission. The director, Wil Lou Gray, had come to Winthrop College, my alma mater, to enlist aid. I agreed to go for two months into the foothills of the Blue Ridge Mountains to Jocassee in the northwestern part of the state. A secluded community, most of its people had never been away from it. The minister could read the Bible, but he could not write. The community leader had been drafted into the army, and he, at least, knew something about the outside world. In past years, the teacher was just the best student, whose capabilities were limited to teaching those who wished to learn how to write their names and read a few simple things. The people were naturally skeptical of an outsider.

Nevertheless, the summer turned out to be remarkable. I had to be poled across the river in a small boat each morning to reach the one-teacher schoolhouse, for there was no bridge in that part of the world. There I met a dozen or so eager children of varying ages, bright enough, but, needless to say, of limited experience. They were interested in all the things the outsider had to say about the world they had never seen. They had never seen a train though there was one about twenty miles away. There was simply no transportation in or out of Jocassee. Only the mail carrier had a car; he went once a week to a country store some miles away to pick up mail. He also did the shopping for everyone scattered here and there in the region: not that the men and women wanted much, perhaps a pound of sugar or a yard of calico for a sunbonnet. The people grew their own food and raised cattle, which were driven by the community leader to the

Margaret M. Bryant

nearest small town once a year and sold for a little money.

My summer was not only interesting: it was also rewarding, for it was there that I discovered the dialect of the seventeenth century, preserved because of the seclusion of the community. The colorful expressions intrigued me. Had I had the training in language I now have, I could have written a book about that summer's experience. I did listen carefully, however, and took note of what I was hearing. It was not only the speech habits but the folk customs as well that interested me. I attended my first folk dance there, folk dancing being one of the chief events in the life of the people of Jocassee. Though the time I spent there was short, it undoubtedly sowed the seed which was to sprout and flourish, for, when I returned to college, I pursued studies in language and folklore.

The two months passed quickly and I was off to my next school. To begin as administrator was truly significant, for I learned that the one in charge, to be successful, had to know not only subjects and teach them, but also the other teachers, the students, and the entire community. After that, the years found me in high schools in Kansas, in West Virginia, and, finally, in a private school in New York City, for I had chosen to go to Columbia to work for a master's degree. I worked and saved until I thought I had enough for a year's study at Columbia. Unfortunately, I transferred my money to a bank in South Carolina, and, just a few days before I was to leave for New York, it closed its doors. I was penniless. But I was not to be deterred. I borrowed enough to get to the City and enrolled in the English Department at Columbia.

During that year I worked at all kinds of jobs to make enough to live on and study at the same time. Now, as I look back, I think the loss of my money was really a benefit, for I met many different people in many different stations of life, people who helped me countless ways. I learned not only about New York City but about a world I could not have dreamed of.

After receiving my M.A., I joined the faculty of a small college in North Carolina. For an educator, being in a small college is what being on a small town newspaper is for a journalist. I became well acquainted with my colleagues; I was constant counsellor, for the students were always around. Nevertheless, I

189

found time to continue my French studies and to take a class in the then popular art of china painting. My fifty pieces of china bear witness.

It was a profitable year, but I had decided to return to Columbia. I joined the staff at Hunter College, at that time a tuition-free city institution of 17,000 girls. Dr. Blanche Colton Williams, known for her work with the short story as well as her studies in Anglo-Saxon, had become head of the English Department. As soon as I was hired, she said, "Now, I want you to get a Ph.D." So, for the next few years, I taught in the evening and summer sessions at Hunter and studied at Columbia for my doctorate. For the M.A. degree I had specialized in the Middle English period and nineteenth-century literature, writing my thesis on Tennyson. Now, however, I realized that it was the English language itself that held me fascinated. One of my professors was a pioneer in linguistics, George Philip Krapp. Once he read in class a letter from a lawyer seeking an opinion on the use of *to* in a will — whether it was inclusive or exclusive in meaning. After class, I suggested to Professor Krapp that, for my dissertation, I investigate the meaning of words in legal cases. He was encouraging but said he knew nothing about law. He sent me, however, to law professors, who thought the research extremely difficult to undertake. But I convinced them of my commitment and, at length, one of the professors showed me how to use the law library. The rest was left to me and the result was *English in the Law Courts: The Legal Decisions That Turned on Articles, Prepositions, and Conjunctions*, published by Columbia University Press. It was a study in semasiology — a study of form words: *a*, *an*, and *the*; *through*, *on*, and *by*; *as*, *but*, and *if*.

Never had I dreamed of writing and publishing a book when I contemplated teaching. Nor in my younger days could I have imagined that I would some day be called on by lawyers to give my opinion on certain words or phrases or be asked to appear in court to testify as an authority on words. But it has happened. All of this grew out of hearing a letter read in class. One never knows how far the rippling of the waves will go caused by the throwing of a small stone into the sea.

After receiving my degree, I joined the faculty of Brooklyn College, another tuition-free city institution, formed from the

190

Margaret M. Bryant

Brooklyn Branch of City College for men and the Brooklyn Branch of Hunter for women. It became the largest liberal arts college in the United States. How far I had come from the tiny school at Jocassee! I went to Brooklyn College when it opened its doors in 1930 and remained there for forty-one years as teacher at both the undergraduate and graduate levels, and, for a time, I was chairman of the English department. Though most of my experience was at Brooklyn College, Columbia, and the New School of Social Research in New York, I also lectured at the University of Uppsala, the University of Stockholm, Handelshogakolan in Sweden, India, Burma, Thailand, the Philippines, Australia, New Zealand, and Japan.

So much for the narrative of my teaching career, a career before the days of open admissions, of having to work with students unprepared for college work, who have to go into remedial classes to overcome language deficiencies and attempt to achieve college level verbal competence. We are told that some eighty-seven percent of the seventeen-year-olds are functionally literate, that they can read newspapers, instructions for drivers' license tests, and sign their names. But this test of literacy hardly prepares them for college as I knew it.

Some may argue that a public institution of higher learning should educate all the citizenry. But even in a democracy, should everyone go to college? Some come without any tradition of learning or association with books. They have no commitment to the aims of higher education. Nor do they envision the possibilities higher education holds. If these students wish to continue beyond the high school, they should go first to a two-year college, which would afford them a bridge to the senior college. The senior colleges would then be able to maintain standards.

My own training goes back to the days of the so-called basics, where reading, writing, and arithmetic were stressed, along with respect for teachers, obedience, and good manners. Knowing the alphabet served me well and knowing the multiplication tables has kept me from depending on a calculator.

Then, too, I was brought up in a more stable society, quite different from the one in which the students today live. We were prepared for community leadership and participation. Society desired an enlightened citizenry devoted to the public good.

191

Confronting Crisis

Other aims, as job training and self-fulfillment, were subordinate. Today, when thousands are frequently thrown out of work because of new inventions and have to be retrained, job-training and self-fulfillment are uppermost as aims for education in the minds of the young. Eighty percent of the incoming freshmen at Harvard in the fall of 1978 stated that they wished to be doctors or lawyers, manifesting their insistence on career education. Self-fulfillment, or "doing one's thing," is no longer stressed as it was in more prosperous times. Still, there is something to be said for all three aims. Educators have an obligation to develop, as far as possible, well-rounded individuals who can adapt to the sweeping changes that lie ahead, changes that may cause a person to have several careers within a lifetime. Students should, therefore, be prepared psychologically, as far as possible, and this is where the humanities come into the curriculum. We would be blind to overlook the necessity for job specialization, but we would be just as blind to neglect the creative arts to develop the natural affections. Education must produce young men and women capable of accepting the responsibilities our rapidly changing, complex world will impose — and of developing their humanity.

Charles Richard Sanders, born August 14, 1904, in Murfreesboro, Tennessee, lives in Durham, North Carolina. Educated at Emory and the University of Chicago, he pursued an academic career and taught at Duke University from 1937 until retirement. His major research is in nineteenth-century figures: Samuel Taylor Coleridge, Lytton Strachey, and Thomas Carlyle. At present he is planning to write his remembrances of time past, and he shares something of this in his present essay.

C. Richard Sanders

Make Haste Slowly

The qualities of mind and character that the ideal teacher should possess are stability and equanimity, unending growth to make freshness, vitality, variety, and spontaneity possible, a sense of the past to provide intellectual perspective, confidence vested in authority, a sense of values and a concept of excellence to make valid discrimination possible, catholicity of taste, an interest in and respect for individuals to avoid judging them in terms of any bed of Procrustes, tolerance and flexibility, impartiality, a disinterested love of truth for its own sake, a sense of humor, courage, perseverance, patience, and warmth for those who are taught. The combination of these is indeed ideal; my readers doubt whether any one teacher may have all these qualities.

Stability is essential if the teacher is to avoid being blown hither and thither. The active mind requires fixed points to give it security. Only when the mind has such points of reference well established can it enjoy maximum results from freedom of movement. Equanimity, which allows us to be buffeted by the whirlwind without being overcome, results from achieving a balance between stability and freedom.

I know the stability that has served me well can be attributed to a happy childhood. Until October 1910, when I had

195

just passed my sixth birthday, our family lived in the last house on the left of North Church Street in Murfreesboro, Tennessee. The street came to a dead end just beyond our home, where there was a gate leading into an estate of about twenty acres. It had a long, yellow, river-gravel driveway winding up to a large, two-story, red-brick mansion, with tall white columns in front and on one side, and with towering hickories, oaks, and magnolias around it. There were lilacs and white crepe myrtles near the front. A carpet of lush bluegrass under the trees flowed down hill to Maple Street, a full city block away. The house, built by a merchant named Carney before the Civil War, was torn down in 1910 and the estate cut up into building lots. Several of the big trees stand yet. Remaining to me is a fine photograph of the house.

The John D. Richardson family lived in the house when I knew it. Long after it was torn down, the place continued to haunt my imagination. It worked its way deep into my subconscious. I never gave it up or the happy experiences associated with it: we children were given free run of the woods, the pasture, the orchard, and even the house; we were served cookies sprinkled with sugar, "tea-cakes" we called them, using the old Southern name, by Miss Mae, the children's aunt. In college I wrote a short story about the house and Miss Mae. The image I hold of the grounds, the house, and the kind people who lived there is as clear now as ever, and this image has become for me a symbol of indestructible stability. It may also have served others in the same way. Andrew Nelson Lytle wrote delightfully about the estate in his *A Wake for the Living*, and William Yandell Elliott, formerly Professor of Political Science at Harvard and advisor to President Eisenhower, spent some years of his childhood and youth there.

We moved to a farm in the autumn of 1910, where my father and mother allowed me to spend a whole year, in which nature did just as she pleased with me, before I went to school. It was a golden year. I spent most of the days playing alone. I planted a flower bed and watched the plants grow. I invented games. My mother read to me: I was impressed by a story about a wasp that mistakenly tried to enter a hornet's nest. The story would be a point of reference for me forever after when the subject of displaced persons would be brought up. When I entered the first grade, I had more confidence than most of the other pupils because of my wonderful year.

A stable mind should not be stagnant or lifeless but should be constantly growing and in some respects changing. It should be like a tree, which has a permanent center but an area of growth near the circumference. In school my mind began to grow.

My first-grade teacher, Miss Eugenia Nielson, taught us phonetics. I can still see the big cards she held up for us to see and make sounds by — as that of a cat making an *f* sound, or a red-hot horse-shoe dipped in water making a hissing *s*.

My third-grade teacher, Miss Mary Lyon, a beautiful young woman who wore pretty clothes, made learning a joy. Children like to have a pretty teacher, especially if she has brains and personal charm. Miss Lyon could be playful and mischievous too. Sometimes she would sit in the same desk with me and tease me by displaying her gold wrist-watch where I could glimpse it and then before I could read the time, slyly turning her pretty arm.

Miss Lucy Alexander, who taught me in the fourth grade, was a strict disciplinarian, very much in earnest. Once you studied geography and the multiplication tables under Miss Alexander, you would never forget them. Appealing to fourth-graders, and especially to me, was her reading table loaded with books in one of the front corners of the room. After you had finished your lessons, you could go to the table, get a book, and carry it back to your desk. I made many a trip to that table, and, I believe, read every book there. I spent so much time reading that some of my distant kin who preferred manual labor and physical activities declared me "lazy." It was Professor John M. Manly who finally exonerated me when, in graduate school, he spoke of the importance of continued reading and the sense of power good books bring to the reader.

After Miss Lyon and then Miss Helene Hudson in the fifth grade (she was also pretty, wore pretty clothes, and was charming), my year in the sixth grade was dismal. The teacher was unattractive. Stodgy. Dull. With her the whole year was a succession of dud days.

Next year the wind blew in a different direction. I was

moved ahead to the eighth grade. To this day I do not know whether the move was a wise one. I floundered badly. But a bright light appeared: a redheaded firebrand, Miss Clark, whose scorching tongue kept the most undisciplined boys in a state of fear. One day she lined us up against the wall and fired questions at us. I expected the worst as she worked her way down the line. Suddenly she skipped six or seven others and asked me I-don't-know-what question. Nor do I know what I replied, but she liked my answer for she said, "This boy has a mind as quick as lightning." From then on I enjoyed her favor and regained my sense of security. It remained with me all through high school.

I am grateful to my teachers of history and literature. The mind that does not have knowledge of the past has no depth and no stance from which to make judgments. Think for a moment what our minds would be like if we had no knowledge of Homer, Plato, Aristotle, Sophocles, Virgil, Horace, Dante, Cervantes, Chaucer, Shakespeare, Milton, and Wordsworth. What a dismal world it would be without them! And to understand Hitler, we need take a look at the tyrants of the East, at Roman Nero, at Frederick the Great, and at Napoleon.

My high school and college experience led me to observe that no two good teachers are alike or use the same methods. James Hinton, a medievalist at Emory, had the most accurate mind I have ever observed. Yet he was neither dogmatic nor pompous but eminently human and kind. Deeply emotional, he would weep over the death of Desdemona. He was a kind of field general, a little Napoleon, who directed research with enthusiasm, diligence, and precision; and with equal enthusiasm, diligence, and precision surveyed the field and his wide circle of friends all over the United States to find jobs for his students.

Thomas H. English, a gentleman with exquisite taste, had a classroom style brilliantly aphoristic and epigrammatic. He knew how to make wise use of silence, sometimes sitting several minutes without uttering a word while students thought their own thoughts and waited for the pin to drop, when almost explosively out would come a striking comment that reopened the discussion.

Until now I have spoken almost altogether of helpful people and positive forces and have said little about negative ones.

198

C. Richard Sanders

There were some. Compulsory ROTC, for one. The itchy, hot, woolen leggings we had to wear under a blazing sun, the senseless drilling and maneuvering we had to go through, the requirement to take a machine gun to pieces, oil it, and reassemble it in perfect order, the sham warfare — none of these things brought any nurturance to my mind. And, like James Thurber, I suffered through science courses. I could not see what I was supposed to see under the microscope. To make matters worse, I could not draw.

More guidance in course selection would have helped me. Some of the courses I took in education and sociology were a pure waste of time. I needed to be directed into courses in German, Greek, and more Latin. Nothing has done more to increase my command of English and to sharpen my linguistic sense than moving back and forth from one language to another in the exercise of translation. One summer I studied *Beowulf* under Kemp Malone. I wrote out and polished my translation as if I would publish it. It does not really matter that I never did.

I am not at all sure just how music and the fine arts are related to my list of qualities for the ideal teacher. They are related to whatever is vitalizing, relaxing, discriminating, and humanizing. I have loved music. I have played — the saxophone, the flute. I have sung — with the glee club. I ushered at every opera that the Metropolitan brought to Atlanta. Caruso had just died, but Gigli, Bori, Martinelli, and Chaliapin still sang.

When I left Emory for the University of Chicago, I felt only continuity, thanks to James Hinton's enthusiasm for research and high standards. I was extremely fortunate to study with John M. Manly, George Sherburn, Ronald S. Crane, Robert Morse Lovett, Fred Millet, and J. R. Hulbert. Some of us were allowed to work with Manly on his text of the *Canterbury Tales*, and we were delighted when Miss Edith Rickert would come into the large room where we worked. Seating herself opposite Manly, she asked him questions and drew out the riches of his mind. We would stop to listen. This was a feast of reason and a flow of soul. At times Miss Rickert would tell us details concerning the personal idiosyncrasies of the monks who had produced the eighty-odd manuscripts with which we worked. She had a remarkable gift for discovering what the old scribes were like by reading between lines and observing the extent to which they did or did not take liberties or be careless with the text they copied.

Sherburn was the least stuffy of all the good teachers I have had. He was also the most accommodating. Within a week after I had enrolled in his eighteenth-century seminar he had carried me in his own automobile across the city to show me how to use the Newberry library. His teaching was human, vital, and spontaneous.

Ronald S. Crane, when I knew him, was still primarily concerned like A. O. Lovejoy, with whom he corresponded, with the history of ideas. In one of his seminars I was audacious enough to offer to make a study of primitivism in Goldsmith, on whom he was an authority. I was surprised and delighted when he offered to let me use his personal library, for he had a reputation for being aloof, mechanical, and exacting with his students. I am deeply grateful to him for increasing my interest in the history of ideas and for teaching me effective techniques for dealing with them. He had mastered the art of teaching, and I was sorry that he gave up teaching for the study of aesthetics and critical values later.

Lovett was more concerned about the condition of society than about literature, and he would say that all the great critics and teachers moved from criticism of literature to criticism of life. A friend of Jane Addams, he had lodgings at Hull House, and was the least belletristic of all my teachers. It was at his suggestion and under his direction that I wrote my dissertation on Coleridge and the Broad-Church Movement, a fertile field in which to work.

Fred Millett awakened my interest in Bloomsbury, and, as I read from Lytton Strachey, Virginia Woolf, and E. M. Forster, the catholicity of my mind was indeed broadened.

Next to Sherburn, the kindest professor I had at Chicago was J. R. Hulbert. I took his course in Middle English dialects by correspondence, but actually the postal service was not used, for I was teaching a course at Chicago and had an office next to his. Twice a week I would take him the work I had done and pick up the next assignment. His written comments were generous, his conversation more so. One day he surprised me, "How late do you work at night, Sanders?" I replied that I almost never worked after eleven o'clock. He then said that I worked too much, that I should not work at night, that Manly and Sherburn did not, and that I should relax at night. I could hardly believe what I had heard. Yet in the back of my mind appeared the thought of a friend who had shortly before suffered a nervous breakdown in the Harvard graduate school.

My first teaching was at Baucom, a country community on the high tableland called "The Barrens" just west of the Cumberland Mountains in Tennessee. Nine miles from the nearest railway and paved road, Baucom lay halfway between Wartrace and Manchester. The school had ten grades and four teachers. At nineteen, with two years of college behind me (I had withdrawn from college because of typhoid fever), I was principal — and teacher of the eighth, ninth, and tenth grades. I taught fifteen classes a day, everything from agriculture to Cicero. I conducted chapel exercises, coached basketball teams for both girls and boys, directed the school play (the parents would not allow me to put make-up on the girls' faces), held the annual ice-cream festival for the town, and for weeks had to attend revival services in nearby churches whenever the occasion arose. Four of the boys were about my age. I made friends with three of them, partly by allowing them to chew their tobacco under the big chestnut trees across the dusty road during recess. The fourth was more difficult. When I called a foul on him on the outdoor basketball court, he drew a knife on me. I expelled him. A few weeks later I punished his cousin for unruliness. Soon afterwards, as I walked the mile and a half to my lodgings, the boy I had expelled and a friend confronted me, showering me with curses and threats. The next day I borrowed a horse and rode down the ravine to the hollow five miles away where the family of the boy I had punished lived. I knew I could have been sniped at from the brush and trees along the road, but I had to take the bull by the horns. The father was reasonable enough. We talked for some time, and I rode back to my lodging, satisfied that I would have no more trouble. Another time an angry father threatened me with a beating, saying that I interfered with his rights because I enforced my rule against tardiness in dealing with his three daughters. My three friends sat on the front steps of the school, whittling and watching, all the while the father raved. He was no fool; he cooled off quickly.

Memories of Baucom have been pleasant, however, partly because of the simple pleasure of picking up chestnuts along the road as I walked to and from school (chestnuts are now almost impossible to find, the trees having died from blight in the early 1930s) and partly because I encountered difficulties there that would make later problems seem much less formidable. Baucom fortified my courage.

In 1927, I received my M.A. degree from Emory and went to teach in Peacock School for Boys on Peachtree Street in Atlanta. The students were a strange combination of boys considered by their parents too bright to attend public school, boys who had special problems, or those who were slow to learn. Once, when I punished a boy for a breach of discipline, his parents appeared, the mother insisting that I apologize. I countered with the demand that the boy apologize to me before the class. The father supported me. The boy apologized. But we never know just whom we teach. One of the older boys in the class, well-disciplined, neatly dressed, and studious, joined another boy in the killing of a drugstore clerk. There was no robbery, no motive. The boys were from wealthy families. They had committed murder for the thrill.

Two experiences stand out in my mind in relation to perseverance and patience. One is the memory of plowing a ten acre field on my father's farm when I was about fifteen. I walked behind a moldboard plow pulled by two horses. To watch the soil ripple over the shining surface of the plow and respond to its motion was pleasurable. But like a dark cloud the thought would come that I would need to walk hundreds of such furrows to finish the plowing. The task seemed endless, overwhelming. But, knowing the job had to be done, I replaced my dissatisfaction with the thought that I was really making one long circling furrow which coiled snugly beside itself again and again and must surely end in a completely plowed field. I have retained this image through the years, along with something Mrs. Richardson said to my mother once, "Brick upon brick and precept upon precept, you will succeed if you are patient. . . ." I associate perseverance also with my high school algebra and geometry classes, when I faced problems that seemed impossible to solve.

But I refused to be defeated; I worked for hours to experience my small moments of victorious exultation.

But this is no perfect success story. Perhaps I should not have expelled the boy at Baucom who drew his knife on me. Instead, I should have tried to help him. Possibly some students cannot be helped beyond a certain point, but I am now convinced — after forty-three years of teaching at Emory, Chicago, and Duke — that we should always go the extra mile in the exercise of patience.

The good teacher will aim as high as he can; even if he or she aims above the ability of the best, all the students will be forced to reach upward, and it is this stretch that is so important in the learning process. A democracy must have leaders, and it is the business of the college to produce these leaders, as Woodrow Wilson insisted, to educate them. They will not be educated if the level of the process is that of the middle or lower group. The present-day emphasis on students of the lower group can only result in the drift toward mediocrity that de Tocqueville in the early nineteenth century feared would develop in the United States. If we do not educate for leadership, as Oxford and Cambridge have always tried to do, then we have no complaint to register about the quality of leadership in our public figures.

The good teacher will realize the care that goes into the choice of texts. Both teacher and student should be provided with an authentic text, a critical edition, with notes to throw light on factual matters, with glosses for difficult words and translations for passages in foreign languages. It should not interpret the work, for interpretation is a prerogative and pleasure that belongs to the teacher and the student. C. E. Ward and I agreed on these ideals for editing an abridgment of Sir Thomas Malory's *Le Morte Darthur* with introduction and notes. We present the late fifteenth-century Caxton text, stripped of digressions, divided into chapters and paragraphs, with quotations marked as such and with difficult vocabulary glossed, so that the work reads as a novel, and the student may discover first-hand the glories of medieval romance as well as the nature of the English language before Shakespeare and the King James translation of the Bible.

The good teacher will use a grading system based on valid

Confronting Crisis

discrimination, indispensable in a democracy. Such a system requires the teacher be courageous, judicious, and constantly on
guard against political influence. If a student receives merely
"passing" or "failing" as a grade, or if he is graded in terms not
relevant, he has not received justice. A democracy cannot continue without justice, and justice cannot exist without valid discrimination. The assignment of grades affords the teacher a test
for determining his or her ability to make discriminating judgments.

Finally, there is disinterestedness, a goal too often ignored
by college personnel — and the politically involved — who tell
the students that they should face the problems of society. The
advice seems plausible, but I take my stand with Coleridge in
Biographia Literaria, with John Henry Newman in "The Idea of
a University," and with Matthew Arnold in *Culture and
Anarchy*. All three teach that the student should withdraw for a
time from efforts to apply his ideas and his ideals until the mind
has had a chance to mature. For the student must learn to love
truth for the sake of truth and not for the sake of some immediate application of it to the problems of society. The student
reformer may do more harm than good, for his ideas may be
half-baked. Let us contrast Shelley and Milton. Shelley was a
rebel, a reformer, and an activist while still in college. And, even
though he wrote "Prometheus Unbound," there are critics who
maintain his poetry to be thin and unsubstantial, who insist that
he remained an adolescent. John Milton, on the other hand,
read, wrote poetry, and enjoyed music while at Cambridge and
for six delightful years at Horton, his father's quiet country estate. After a jolly tour of the continent, he was ready when he
returned home for the life that lay ahead as Cromwell's Latin
Secretary, the chief "activist," and master polemicist in English
literature. In one of his sonnets he speaks of the slow maturing of
his mind, which he did not allow to be distorted by too early efforts at reform.

Festina lente ("Make haste slowly"), said one of the Roman
emperors, placing the admonition on the coins of the empire.
Hundreds of years later, Thomas Carlyle, preaching his dynamic
gospel of work, repeated the phrase many times. We read in
Hudibras, "A slow fire makes sweet malt," my final message in
this essay for both the teacher and the student.

204

Jesse Hilton Stuart, born August 8, 1907, near Greenup, Kentucky, worked as farmer, newspaper editor, steel mill laborer, teacher, and superintendent of schools before being recognized as a creative writer. He is perhaps best known for *Man with a Bull-Tongue Plow* (verse, 1934), *Taps for Private Tussie* (1943), and *The Thread That Runs so True* (1949). His characters have been termed homespun and heart-warming. Once labeled condescendingly a regionalist, he has lived to see that title respected and his own genius termed local colorist with universal appeal. Of the contribution Mr. Stuart has made to this book, he writes, "I believe it might be my best. . . ."

To Teach, To Love

Today it is a shocking fact that in America approximately forty-eight percent of our elementary and secondary pupils drop out of school before they reach or finish the twelfth grade. Parents, teachers, and the general public are alarmed. In my state of Kentucky the dropout figures are much higher than the national average. We have, according to reports, approximately a sixty-five percent dropout. Educators are trying to learn the causes in order to effect some sort of cure. And they are finding the going difficult. They have suggested that the age limit of compulsory school attendance be raised two more years. Some of our people who believe money is a cure-all for all problems pay their children to go to school with bonus bribes for passing simple high-school courses and additional bonuses for higher grades.

Now, the reasons parents too often give for their children's leaving school is that the teachers are inefficient or the school plants are inadequate, or the cafeteria food isn't any good. Sometimes it is that "old mean teacher" who fails everybody. Very often parents will come to the school (at least they did when I was principal) and demand that teachers "up" the grades so their children can pass. One year in a local high school parents tried to sue two teachers who failed to pass a boy and a girl in a

207

subject, which kept them from graduating. One of these teachers was my youngest sister. Since local attorneys would not take these suits, the parents went to a large city and sought the advice of attorneys there. Failing again, they took their charges against these teachers to the state Department of Education, who passed the buck back to the county superintendent and local school board. This is an indictment of our people. It also has a demoralizing effect upon our teachers. But the sorry attitude of a minority of parents is not the single cause of such a high percentage of dropouts.

I have spent the best years of my life as a classroom teacher or as a school administrator. These years, for the most part, have been spent in secondary schools, and I have come to know the secondary pupils very well. And to know them is to love them, regardless of their virtues or faults. The so-called "teen-age" years are, in my estimation, the most wonderful years in the life of man. I have heard silly people condemn and bemoan this age, but there isn't a week in my life that I do not wish to return to it. And this is a wonderful time for teachers and parents to mold and shape adolescents into useful men and women.

It is most unfortunate that American parents who blame teachers, school plants, cafeteria food, and other things for their children's dropping out of school cannot travel to some other countries just to learn about the general superiority of American teachers and American schools. We Americans are prone to boast about having the best of everything. We can truly boast of telephones, bathtubs, automobiles — gadgets that make life easier, more comfortable, and softer. However, we can no longer boast of the better automobile, for the German, British, Italian, French automobiles are replacing our cars over the world. We can no longer compete in some areas of world trade. There are other commodities which we used to export that have been replaced, mainly by Japanese and German competition.

But there are professions in which we are at least a half-century ahead of the world average. American-trained schoolteachers, doctors, dentists, nurses, health officers, engineers, and agricultural technicians are in demand over all the world, except in a few European countries; our agricultural technicians have worked in nearly all of the countries overseas.

208

My students who were trained in agriculture in our county high school could serve as agricultural technicians and soil conservationists in many of the seventy-four countries I have visited.

The fundamental philosophy of our public schools is "the greatest good for the greatest number" and "educating for their needs." This is a sound philosophy that has paid dividends. Each youth is entitled to a free education up through twelve grades; he is not only free to go, but compelled to attend up to a certain age. In addition to this great public school system, there are excellent private and church schools all over the United States. There is no question that we have the finest school system on earth. Then why do we have forty-eight percent dropouts?

Perhaps Americans who have taught in American-sponsored missionary universities, college, secondary and elementary schools overseas are better qualified to answer this question than teachers who have taught only in the United States. American doctors, nurses, agricultural experts, building technicians, and Peace Corps members should have some excellent answers. And I believe the answers from all of these groups might have a common denominator. But first, let me admit that after teaching a year in the American University in Cairo, Egypt, I have almost become a "spoiled" American teacher. I have changed my ideas about begging students in America to finish high school and college. They should, if they have any sense at all, know the value of an education, of head or hand or a combination of the two.

When I went to the American University in Cairo I couldn't conceive of their having a wall around the campus, a large gate and padlock where a bowab (keeper of the gate) allowed the students and teachers to go through only upon identification. Everybody wanted to go to the American University, which was staffed with teachers from ten countries, American and Egyptian teachers in the majority.

My students were eager. They asked me questions that were hard to answer. With the exception of three American students and one Canadian, not one of my students spoke fewer than three languages. I learned that their being able to speak, write, and understand English was the main criterion of their acceptance; that of every six who applied, only one was chosen. Here

209

were the best and most eager students I ever taught in my life. The schoolteacher was the most respected person on earth. They were especially fond of American teachers. A few Americans among us would not be considered outstanding teachers in American schools, but they were considered wonderful there. A lemon teacher in America is a sweet apple over there.

The majority of the students were Muslims. If anybody ever taught better students than the Greeks and Armenians (who are of minority Christian groups in a Muslim country) or Muslim girls, who for the first time are beginning to fill the colleges and universities, I would like to listen to that teacher. "Dropouts," unless because of sickness or poverty, are unheard of there. These youth will fight to get into school. When the teacher walks through the gate onto the campus, the students stand. The graduates of this small school in Cairo who receive scholarships for America go to such institutions as Harvard, Yale, M.I.T., Columbia, Vanderbilt, University of Chicago, Princeton, Duke, Emory, University of Illinois, Indiana University, Ohio State, University of Iowa, University of California, and the University of Minnesota. Secondary schools are few and far between in Egypt. Most of the students I taught had been educated in missionary schools: Presbyterian, Catholic, Orthodox, Coptic, Greek, and Armenian. They go anywhere they can to a secondary school. So the Egyptian youth cannot understand "dropouts." The whole populace would be educated in a few years if they had our school system in Egypt.

From September 1962 until February 1963, I went around the world as a specialist for the United States Information Service (USIS), a branch of the State Department. I lectured to university, college, and secondary-school groups, to teacher and writing groups in Iran, Egypt, Greece, Lebanon, West Pakistan, East Pakistan, the Philippines, Taiwan (Formosa), and Korea. I learned much about the young people by talking directly with them and with their teachers. Although I imparted knowledge to them, I received more from them than I gave. Poor as these countries were by our American standards, these millions — yes, a billion people — were on the rise. And they are working first to equal and then to surpass America. It was a thrilling experience to see them advance and to note how proud they were of their small achievements.

There were conditions that broke my heart too in these countries. Youth were crying to go to elementary schools, to secondary schools, to colleges and universities. There were not enough schools and teachers to accommodate those eager for an education.

All we need to do is to give these eager young people teachers. Let the physical plants come later. American parents, never satisfied, who complain about the schools and teachers, should see what the American teacher can do for the unspoiled and bright children of other lands. If the youth of these countries where I visited had American teachers, with a hot lunch thrown in free, there would not be even three percent dropouts. Can any American doubt the integrity of young people who sit on the doorstep of a school that is bursting at the seams, waiting for a student to move away or die so they can fight for his place?

I do not mean this to wind up a heavy-breathing advertisement for the American teacher. Teacher strikes leave me cold, in fact downright freezing — though I believe in the union and how it has helped raise teachers' salaries. I scorn graduate degrees earned merely to raise the pay another notch. Teachers who don't have the calling aren't worth your good tax dollar — and I use the word "calling" in the old-fashioned pulpit sense. A good teacher has either to love his kids or his subject. A great teacher loves both and marries the two. As the spirit has seeped out of the schools, teacher attitudes have changed.

So what has happened to our people in America? Why do we have almost fifty percent dropouts before our young people reach the twelfth grade? It cannot be denied in America that our main motive in education is to "make life easier." We have tried to replace all labor with machines, even machines to think for us. We have even tried to invent a teaching machine to replace the teacher. We have mechanical slaves to do ninety percent of our work. Each day we read in the papers, or hear over the radio, or see on TV that some person has devised a way by which one man can do the job of twenty.

We read or hear daily that our country is heading toward socialism. That isn't true; we're not heading that way, for we are already there. There's not another country in this world where the supposedly poor can drive automobiles to haul their free commodities home. Some of the people who don't work live about as well as some who do. In New York City alone we have a million people on welfare.

No wonder our youth drop out of school! What is there for them out there in our bleak future? Why become a number, a zip code, a cipher? This new way of life is tearing the very guts and hearts out of our youth, deadening their brains, killing the greatest inheritance a youth can have, incentive to do, incentive to have, incentive to compete. We look askance at people who are eager to work, who like to save, to build fortunes. We have a name for these people: Eager Beavers! We soft-pedal competition. Yet competition, academic and athletic, is present in every country on earth. Americans love to compete, and millions pay to see them compete.

In the Kentucky mountains some have drawn their dole so long, they perhaps will never work again. They don't know how!

What do you think has happened to their children who attend public schools? What ambition will they have? When a tree fell across the road, we used to take axes and saws, maybe a mule team or a tractor, and remove the tree. Today we call the state Department of Highways. So what is so strange about youth's demanding unearned grades from teachers so they can graduate?

When they look into the future, what do they see? Is it better to work or not work? It doesn't matter much, for if they don't work they may fare about as well as those who do. Incentive, ambition, and competition are almost archaic words in our language. Our present and future generations will demand and get as long as we can give, while the pauper countries of the world, whose youth are eager to rise, will work and rise up like long-submerged islands in the sea. My father used to say the third generation was a shirt-sleeve generation. The first generation worked to make it, the second generation spent it, and the third generation were in shirt sleeves again. Will our future generations be shirt-sleeve generations?

In our Kentucky area this summer twelve thousand youth applied for work to help them defray college expenses. Of this number, only eleven hundred got work. These were the ambitious ones. Tell youth something is out there for them if they will only work for it, and ninety percent of them will. Yet, we haul them free to school by bus. We give them a free noon meal if they can't pay for it. We buy their books, and we pass laws to protect them from labor. We give them everything, even money to stay in school and money to make grades. We try to buy them. Money can't turn the trick.

We forget the human spirit and its response to challenge. We have forgotten incentive and competition. These are dirty words, but how the people of the world love them. A Greek girl I taught at the American University in Cairo couldn't get a scholarship (she couldn't get money out of Egypt) to come to America. I thought she was a good student, although she didn't have the best grades there, and I recommended her for a scholarship, which she didn't get. She actually begged me to say a kind word for her in America, and I did. An institution of higher learning accepted this twenty-one-year-old girl, who had taught school one year for a pitifully low wage. All she could do was pay her way over and bring a few clothes. She was ambitious and determined. Of the eleven grades she received, nine were A's and two were B's. She got her M.A. degree in one year, youngest in the class of 275, and with the highest grades.

This is the spirit of youth. Give them a challenge, and they accept it. They want to work. They want to do. Give each boy and girl a goal to work for; give him or her a challenge, and I'll guarantee that only sickness or death will make him or her drop out of school. We might even equal or surpass Japan's record of 99.7 percent that remain to finish the free elementary and junior high schools.

And the purpose of education must not be purely materialistic. It must not have value only in dollars and cents.

My purpose in going to college was not to expand my earning power. I had teachers who taught me that knowledge was the greatest thing I could possess, that a college education would awaken the kingdom within me — help me expand my heart, mind, and soul.

Then there was my father. "Amount to something," he often said. And my mother once told us: "I want you children to live so I will never be ashamed of a one of you. And you, Jesse, I

Confronting Crisis

want you to amount to so much that when you are in a crowd, you will be singled out and someone will say: 'He's Martha Hilton's son.' " I never forgot her words.

There were many things between me and my college. The main one was dollars.

But I pursued my dream, and I learned both in and out of the classroom. For one thing, I learned to apply Ralph Waldo Emerson's kind of self-reliance I had read about in high school. Somehow, I learned that most men sometime must accept defeat. I wanted a first place on our track team, but never got it. But I learned if one wanted a first place in something that he could not get, the next best thing was to try to excel at something else.

In August 1969, forty years will have passed since I received my diploma at Lincoln Memorial. Was the seedbed carefully prepared in college? What of the harvest?

Materially, I have done better than ever I expected. My birthplace was a one-room shack; as an itinerant farm-boy worker, I earned twenty-five cents a day. Now I live in a comfortable home and own the farms where my father and mother rented and sharecropped in my youth, a thousand acres in all. I have made over one hundred thousand dollars in one year. But these are not the important things. They are the by-products of my dream — education and enlightenment, and awakening of the kingdom within.

As a teacher, I have tried to go beyond the textbooks into the character — stressing honesty, goodness, and making each life count for something. I have written thirty-two books, nearly four hundred short stories, two hundred articles and essays, and two thousand poems, trying to share my dream. I have tried to arouse and awaken our people through more than five thousand lectures. I shall do more.

Surely, I owe more than mere gratitude for God-given talents and energy and for the privileges, opportunities, and freedom this country has given me to develop them. And the only way I can repay my debt is to work with children. No joy runs deeper than the feeling that I have helped a youth stand on his own two feet, to have courage and self-reliance, and to find himself when he did not know who he was or where he was going.

214

Yes, I have tried to follow my dream — and it has led me to dedicate much of my life to an effort to be an awakening teacher, one like so many of those I knew in my own youth, like so many of those who taught me and, later, studied under me.

Let me tell you about one more such teacher.

When eighty-four percent of the Greenup Countians voted to eliminate sixty-six rural schools for ten consolidated ones, Nina Mitchell Biggs was one of the dissenting sixteen percent.

Nina Mitchell Biggs, a former teacher, taught her first school in Greenup County in 1881. She was fifteen in 1881 when she taught the Raccoon Rural School.

She taught big boys, too, but discipline wasn't her problem. Her problem was keeping the sheep out of her school.

Colonel Bill Worthington, lieutenant governor when William O. Bradley was governor, had purchased the denuded acres that made up the entire Raccoon-Furnace area. Colonel Bill figured the best thing to do with his newly acquired acres was to raise sheep.

When he clashed with the spirited fifteen-year-old teacher Miss Nina Mitchell, Colonel Bill was a man of state and national reputation, attorney, political figure, soldier, and dominant personality. That didn't keep Miss Nina from using the broom more than once on his sheep. She wouldn't let him use her school for a barn.

Miss Nina continued teaching until she married Maurice Biggs in 1886. She moved onto her husband's farm, which was a part of the Biggs's family estate. Nearly seventy years later, long after a bond issue was voted by Greenup Countians to build consolidated schools, Miss Nina, long a widow of great wealth, was forced to leave the home where she had lived almost three-quarters of a century. Industry had taken the acres the Biggs family had owned since the Indians had been chased out by the white settlers.

Within a quarter of a mile stood the neglected Frost School, its pupils transported by bus to the big consolidated McKell Elementary.

Miss Nina could have purchased the finest home in Fullerton or South Shore, but she had another idea. The acre where the Frost School stood reverted to her estate when the school

215

was discontinued, so she purchased the old schoolhouse. She employed two carpenters. Miss Nina and her daughter stood by directing the work.

They built a new home over and around the Frost schoolhouse. Her daughter, Mrs. King, drew the plans.

"I'll see that this one-room school doesn't go," Miss Nina said. "I hate to see the old schools go. But most of them have and we have lost something. I associate them with the old McGuffey Readers. They will live forever with me."

The old one-room Frost School became Miss Nina's living room. Visit her and she'll point out to you where her desk used to be. She'd show you where so-and-so used to sit and now he has retired from business in Ashland or Lexington.

She had memories of her pupils — where they sat in the room and how they played on the schoolground, which is now her yard.

When her former pupils came back to see her they visited their elementary alma mater too. When her own children, now grandparents and great-grandparents, returned, it was alma-mater homecoming for them and for Miss Nina, who was still spry and chipper at ninety-two.

She was determined not to let what she believed in pass away. She was determined to hold on to her rural school so long as she lived.

In Kentucky today, the one-room school, where teachers taught all eight grades, belongs to an age gone by. In portions of our state, especially in the eastern Kentucky mountains, we held on to the one-room school longer than any other state in America, unless it was the mountain areas in West Virginia, Tennessee, Virginia, North Carolina, northern Georgia, and northern Alabama. Still in the mountains of eastern Kentucky and West Virginia there are areas which are using the one-room schools. These schools are in isolated mountain areas where modern highways have not penetrated, where youth cannot be transported by bus to consolidated schools.

Now, in Greenup County, Kentucky, our pupils have been transported by bus to consolidated schools for years. There used to be eighty-two one- and two-room schools in Greenup County, and now only two of these are left. One, the Claylick School

Building, which I visited as a young county school superintendent back in 1932, is still left standing because Greenbo State Park has purchased the grounds. This schoolhouse is now a showplace. And the other is Cane Creek School, where my sister Sophia began teaching at seventeen. Older people with a nostalgic longing for the past drive to this school, sit in parked cars, look at it, and dream. They get out of their cars and look in the windows at the potbellied stove, which is going to rust, and at a few of the old seats that are still left.

These people fondly remember the age gone by. And I remember the years gone by too. I remember them so well that with the permission of the Greenup County school superintendent I hauled the old seats where my pupils sat in 1923 to a building on my farm, where I have them stored. On many of the seats I have found carved initials. I am glad they are on the seats now, but it wouldn't have done for me to have caught a pupil carving his initials on a seat in 1923. Initials are all that a few of these youngsters left to remember them by. In this landlocked and poor rural area, youth back in 1923 had little chance of higher education or making a mark in life. They had such small chance of improving themselves. Today they have equal chances with youth over most of this country.

Now with highways penetrating approximately ninety percent of what used to be inaccessible mountain areas, school buses can haul pupils to large consolidated schools. This new consolidated school, with better-educated and more-sophisticated teachers, superior health practices, and more recreational opportunities, is quite a contrast to the old one-room school. One teacher can teach his or her particular grade or specialty without other pupils listening in. Often one grade is divided and subdivided and there are several teachers. And there is a principal, an assistant principal, and a second assistant principal, not one of whom teaches a class; there is a guidance counselor who doesn't teach but who steers pupils in the right direction according to the results of his testing. We used to talk about Big Business! Now we have to talk about Big Schools. They are going to get bigger, no matter what we say.

Maybe there is a reason why people today in our area and others have a nostalgic feeling for the one-room school, which has disappeared into that bygone era of American life, like the oxcart, sled, saddle, horse and buggy, rubber-tired fringed surrey, jolt wagon, express wagon, hug-me-tight, and the bulltongue, cutter, bottom, and hillside turning plows. Even the passenger trains are going, and we are taking to wings and to three cars a family on the broad highways that thread this nation.

The one-room school had some advantages which the consolidated school cannot give its pupils. One was walking to and from school. Then, the roads were not crowded with automobiles. We walked over hills and up and down valleys where there were only footpaths. And in July, when our country school began, we walked barefoot along the dusty footpaths. We got caught in summer rainstorms. Often we got soaked. We waded streams barefoot. We got to know the names of wildflowers, shrubs, different species of trees. We had books in school (very few), but there was another kind of book all of us had to read, Earth's Book, which was filled with many pages of many delightful paragraphs.

Autumn along these paths was more interesting. The acorns dropped like big brown heavy raindrops from the oaks; the chestnuts dropped to the leafy ground from their satiny burrs that pricked our bare feet. The papaws ripened after the first frost. And the trees were loaded with persimmons, which we tried to get before the possums got them. Then, there were hickory-nut trees everywhere. Mornings we left home very early to try to beat other pupils who traveled the same path to the chestnut trees, papaw groves, and hickory-nut trees. We didn't race for the persimmon trees, for there was always an abundance of this ripened fruit on the ground. We couldn't pick all that fell from the trees. We gathered white and black walnuts and cracked them between rocks under the trees.

I remember animal and bird tracks in the snow. Winter was a great time too. I couldn't keep from tracking a rabbit, fox, possum, mink, or weasel even if I was a little late for school. And I learned how hard it was for animals and birds to live in winter on the scanty food left for them, most of which was covered with snow. Many times I tracked a rabbit to a shock of corn on a hill slope which I shook with my hand to watch the rabbit run out. Many times I found a covey of quail hiding under falling grass

218

where they could gather a few weed seeds to eat. I learned a lot about rain and snowstorms that I couldn't have learned on a school bus. But the pupils today who ride school buses are not to blame. This happened in our changing world. We were the more fortunate because we could walk to and from school. Anybody who ever walked to a one-room country school will tell you about his experiences in the schoolroom. These are dear experiences that will never come again. Youths who visit the few old school relics, bird- and bat-filled belfries where there used to be a school bell, who stand and gawk at these relics of the past, do not know what they have missed. No one fought harder than I did to see our one-room schools go in Kentucky and consolidation come. A country must progress and must move from the past into a modern world; our schools had to move in this direction. But this is what we must never forget: There was a day and time when education was considered a priceless gift.

And what is wrong with such an idea today? Such an idea in a youth or a community, a state or a nation, cannot become outdated.

When I make a speech and tell the young today about the teacher who taught all the grades from first to eighth in six hours, many of them laugh. I know what they are thinking. But they do not know what I am thinking, and it is hard for me to tell them. What I believe we had then in the one-room school was what is called today "The Accelerated School Program." If a student was alert and eager to learn, there was no problem. If a student was not alert and eager, to sit in this schoolroom and hear others recite in classes ahead and behind alerted him. He had to learn to study when there were others reciting or had to study at home. When I went from one grade to another in my scanty schooling at Plum Grove, I could have skipped the grade ahead of me. I had already listened to others ahead of me in their recitations and discussions. My brother James, who attended the Plum Grove school, learned so much so quickly that when he was ten years old he entered Greenup High School and finished when he was fourteen. In his last year at Greenup he made all A's and read all the books in the Greenup High School library and many of the encyclopedias.

The youth today who attend departmentalized consolidated

elementary schools should never laugh when they look at one of the one-room schoolhouse relics now on exhibit in state parks. They ought to know what transpired between pupils and teachers in these one-room schools. They served a day and time in America, and they served it well.

One teacher taught all eight grades and usually enjoyed it. At least I did. Education to them and for them was idealistic and the greatest thing they could pass along in life. The children I taught were, more often than not, unspoiled, eager, and ambitious. And they managed to convey the impression that they enjoyed my classroom. Maybe they were faking it — but you know I don't think so.

We've lost something we've got to get back. Not the one-room schoolhouse, but the spirit of the one-room schoolhouse. I am incurably optimistic about young people and have boundless faith in the kind of people who go into teaching. We'll get it back.

Kenneth H. Ashworth, whose *American Education in Decline* (1979) "sounds the alarm to all concerned administrators and teachers in American academia," is Commissioner of Higher Education in Texas, chief executive officer of the Coordinating Board of the Texas College and University System, and he formerly held positions in university administration and in the United States Office of Education. Dr. Ashworth holds a B.A. degree in economics and the Ph.D. degree in the history and philosophy of education from the University of Texas at Austin.

Kenneth H. Ashworth

The Last Best Hope for Quality in Higher Education

For at least a century now philosophers have argued that man is driven far more by custom and conformity to the conventions of society than by choice based on an understanding of self or the true situation of mortal man in the universe. A good case can be made that not only do men so misguide themselves, but so do most of our social institutions, not excepting our colleges and universities. But before making that case, we need to look briefly at how this philosophical argument concerning the individual has affected educational theory and practice at all levels.

Nothing any of us accomplishes is immunized against being undone. The words under the half-sunk and shattered visage in the desert read: "My name is Ozymandias, king of kings: Look on my works, ye Mighty, and despair!" If any person can separate himself from the society of the self-satisfied, which trusts in success, materialism, and organization, and dare to face a dark night of self revelation to acknowledge that he exists by chance for a brief time in an uncertain life, he will see that to be totally absorbed in the scenario society imposes upon him, to become an unthinking role player in the folly of life, is in large part a charade and an escape to deny his own death. To face the reality of his own mortality and to reject the expectation of social

223

conformity, he would recognize that choices and values in life are neither fixed by authority nor self evident. He would see that choices must be made and values must be developed by him in the context of his own existence. He might even find that the hero role he has set for himself or permitted others to foist upon him is misleading him from living his life as he would really wish to live it.

Samuel Johnson in "The Vanity of Human Wishes" wrote:

> Unnumber'd suppliants crowd Preferment's
>   gate,
> Athirst for wealth, and burning to be great;
> Delusive Fortune hears th' incessant call,
> They mount, they shine, evaporate, and fall.

To reject the demand for conformity, to recognize his own mortality, and to move toward greater individuality, a person would acquire a new awareness, a new view of his life, a new vision of the role he is to play, and a new acceptance of the importance of a reasoning and critical life. If he incorporated such a revelation into his being, he would be a new person, a freer agent.

Kierkegaard calls those who are socially bound and conforming, those afraid to live as individuals, those living comfortably tucked inside other people, "inauthentic" people. They do not belong to themselves, but are wholly owned by society. They play standardized roles they have acquired by accident of family and place and time of birth. He points out that only by looking ahead and accepting one's own death can a person truly live as an autonomous individual making meaningful choices rather than merely accepting the limited life thrust upon most of us by an organized and structured society.

Education has at least three responsibilities in response to such a philosophical position. First, it should assist individuals to make the sharp break necessary to reach an awareness of their true state in the universe. Education should prepare students to move smoothly into such a self awareness, into a recognition of their individuality and separateness from organized conventionality. Schooling has been called a process of socialization, and in America this often has meant and still means the acculturation of the young to customs and what often are no more than fads. This is not preparing students for freedom; it is not providing the disquietude necessary to make individuals function by reason and decisions rather than by conditioned responses.

And the third responsibility of education is to prepare people to function in a society where decisions and choices and options make a great deal of difference both to individuals and the entire community.

Now let us turn to observe the impact on education of the point of view argued by the philosophical position I have been discussing. Several of the topics I will touch on were discussed in the preceding papers. There was some reference to the call to emphasize "the basics." I agree that until an individual is functionally literate and can do basic computations there is little hope to expect him to be more than "stolid and stunned, a brother to the ox," "dead to rapture and despair." But these are papers on higher education, and while it may in some current circles seem elitist, in my view there is no place in a true university to commit resources to provide the basics or, to use the present argot, "to remediate" university-level students. Certainly the fundamentals should be provided, but the university is not the social institution to do it. The university should move up to the next level of "the basics." It should provide the essential elements and techniques for the professions and majors so that the graduates are relatively well labeled as to what they have spent a substantial portion of their time studying.

But these are points far subordinate to the greater responsibility of education to prepare individuals to function in a world in which they wish to make independent judgments and choices. It is not sufficient for students to assimilate a point of view which frees them from organized, lock-step conformity; they must have the tools to make their new freedom useful to them and to make them safe for the rest of society. That is, if individuals are encouraged to make free choices, they must also know how to make choices which are not harmful to the society and which enhance the quality of life the individual chooses to live. Therefore, in addition to assisting the thoughtful individual to live daily with his own mortality, education should provide certain accoutrements for a life of untrammeled but premeditated choices.

This educational responsibility is simply this: to go beyond the basics of a degree major or profession and to provide the individual with the ability to reason effectively, with the resources to be imaginative and innovative, and with the capacity for critical analysis. The three points clearly interrelate. Change arising out of imagination must be governed by reason and ordered thinking. The values and order resulting from reason must be subject to criticism or they can become static and authoritarian. None of these functions can be fulfilled without the fundamentals of having access to knowledge and information. Nor do they serve man well without a store of historical and scientific facts. And they are lacking ferment and insight without the arts. But the main point to be made about the impact of the new philosophy upon education is the need for implanting useful and effective habits of the mind along with specific skills, techniques, data, and facts.

All of this should lead us, without surprise, to conclude that the most functional, utilitarian, and necessary part of a higher education is the liberal arts. For there we find the facts, the information, the arts, all of the grist for the application and enhancement of the skills and techniques and "the basics." But above all, we find in the liberal arts the setting to develop the rational, imaginative, and critical habits of the mind essential to the individual bent upon choosing his own course through life to the very end.

Now to return to the case that our social institutions as well as individuals are oriented toward conformity and conventionalism. This is not to be unexpected, since our institutions are creatures of individuals and groups of people and are subject to the pressures applied by other social organizations. Recognizing this propensity of institutions, the universities must work to remain nonconforming and unconventional organizations.

Much that we find in the university environment attests to its differentness from other social institutions. Voting among employees on institutional goals and purposes is unique, as is participation in the selection of leaders at the top and even mid-level positions in the organization. Hiring by peer-group evaluation is almost unheard of elsewhere in society. Academic freedom as a protection for nonconformists is a special recognition not provided in industry or government. The additional guarantee of freedom of speech and tenure to guarantee it are provided in recognition that truth is usually sought by only a few and is rarely revealed to the masses in a single revelation. Therefore, the minority who finds truth early must be protected to keep it from being stamped out. This is why truth is not ruled by majority vote in a university.

Society also has found that the university offers a good place to test changes that are proposed. It is a good place to speculate and to rehearse possible consequences of courses of action before they are tried out in a volatile, real world.

It is also a place where criticism can be tolerated because the university only deals with words and thoughts and not actions. And the university is a place where it is possible to reason out meanings and articulate values transcending the mundane and prosaic and short-term existence.

In addition, since it deals with shaping minds, attitudes, and intellectual habits, it must not be a creature of other institutions or interests in society.

It is for these reasons that the university is not a microcosm of the society. It is not like any other social institution. It stands aside and looks to the past and recognizes the impermanence of all man's creations. It does not conform. It does not seek to be conventional. Were it to follow in lockstep with the other institutions of society, it would lose its uniqueness and fail to justify its own existence. In many ways, the university is the ideal of what the individual should seek to find for himself — a nonconformed, reasoning, imaginative, and critical organism.

Yet we find today that higher education is increasingly being directed by government to conform to social standards which are established outside the colleges and universities. We find the government using higher education as an instrument of social change. At times institutions of higher education become action arms of the government in dealing with specific problems. We see peer-group evaluation and hiring being eroded by government requirements. We see standards of admission and performance lowered in order to satisfy government goals and expectations. And we see the government defining problems and setting goals and timetables for research. Politics is a game of short-term payoffs, and this is often inconsistent with the purposes of higher learning.

Some wag has said that the poor universities change quickly, the better universities change slowly, and the best ones change not at all. While this cannot be accepted as true, it is not without some value as a guide. Change should be accepted gradually and should be tested against what it proposes to replace. In facing social pressures to adjust and accommodate, universities should apply to the efforts to make them conform the same three components required by free-standing individuals: reason, imagination, and criticism. They should work to maintain their freedom from conventionalism and their liberty to make choices affecting their present and future. The foregoing articles all touch in different ways on these points of quality, autonomy, and purpose in our institutions of higher learning.

Our colleges and universities should apply rigorous standards to proposed modifications; otherwise change will lead to chaos and declining quality. Yet we must search for imaginative solutions to problems. That can be done best if the rigors of the reasoning and the fertility of imagination are subjected to the criticism coming from careful analysis and evaluation.

The articles here have contributed to these points, particularly in the teaching role of the colleges and universities. It is important that the teachers show concern over quality control, standards, and purposes in higher education regardless of what their own administrators', the public's, and the government's views may be. For in the end, the faculty is the last best hope for maintaining quality and defining the correct purposes for institutions of higher learning. No orders from however high can command that quality be maintained and improved. For quality control in higher learning resides with the faculties.

Note on the text:

*This book is set in Times New Roman,
10 point type, with italic and bold face characters.
Times Roman was designed for the* London Times
*by Stanley Morison and was first used in 1932.
The text is printed on 60-pound Beckett India vellum;
the cover is Roxite C Linen Finish fabric, gold
foil stamped. Typesetting is by Student Publications,
The University of Texas at Arlington; printing is by
Branch-Smith, Fort Worth; book design
by Jim Nelson Black.*